MOSES

James R. Shott

Illustrated by
Ken Landgraf

BARBOUR
PUBLISHING, INC.
Uhrichsville, Ohio

© MCMXCVIII by Barbour Publishing, Inc.

ISBN 1-57748-176-3

Published by Barbour Publishing, Inc.
        P.O. Box 719
        Uhrichsville, Ohio 44683
        http://www.barbourbooks.com

 Member of the
Evangelical Christian
Publishers Association

Printed in the United States of America.

1

A man sat under a palm tree in a desert oasis, waiting for someone to come. He was thirsty. The well was twenty feet away, but he had no bucket or rope. He hoped someone would come soon.

It was so peaceful here in this quiet oasis. He leaned back against the palm tree and closed his eyes. Soon he dozed in the stillness of the late afternoon.

Voices startled him and he sat up, alert. At last, he would have his drink. He started to get up but changed his mind, remaining hidden behind the palm tree. Something about the voices warned him to be careful.

They belonged to some young men—or boys, judging by their carefree enthusiasm. He recognized the language immediately. His childhood nurse back in Egypt had spoken it. He could understand it, even though these boys had a strange accent.

"Don't come out until my signal!"

"They're coming! Quick! Hide!"

"Don't forget, I want that older girl."

The man under the palm tree grinned to himself.

This should be interesting. He might have to work for his drink.

The young men said nothing more, and the silence became tense. Then came the tinkle of girlish laughter, mingled with the bleating of sheep and the steady drumbeat of their running hooves.

The man shifted his position slightly as he listened. The girlish voices gently scolded the sheep as they crowded around the well. He heard the splash of their goatskin bucket as it dropped. Water gurgled into the stone trough, and the sheep slobbered it greedily. The splashing noises continued. After several dips, the sheep had enough to drink.

Then came the sound he'd been waiting for: a loud "Whooop!" and a patter of feet, as the boys leaped from their hiding places and noisily scattered the frightened sheep. The shrieks of the girls mingled with the taunting laughter of the boys.

The man under the palm tree stood up.

Nobody saw him at first because they had their minds on other things. Quickly he looked around, taking in the situation. Seven girls. Five boys. The oldest boy—the only one with a beard—struggled with the tallest girl, while his four companions threatened the

THE BOYS LEAPED FROM THEIR HIDING PLACES.

other six girls with their staffs. The man frowned. He'd better hurry.

The older boy's arms encircled the tall girl, holding her tightly as he tried to trip her and push her to the ground. He succeeded, but she fought hard—and quietly; the screams came not from her, but from the other girls.

The four boys and six girls, who had been watching the two struggling on the ground, now saw the man step in front of them.

"Let her go!"

The bearded youth on the ground jerked his head around, saw only one man, and grinned. "Take care of him, brothers. I'm busy."

The other four youths glared at the stranger with contempt.

"Look at this, will you? A desert rat just crawled out of his hole."

"Not a rat; a dog. Can't you tell what his father is?"

One of the boys snorted. "Don't insult a dog like that."

They laughed and gripped their staffs, then spread out for battle.

The man moved quickly, as he had been taught in Egypt, his staff thrust forward like a spear. A blur of action

"LET HER GO!"

followed, almost too fast to see. Thud. Thud. Thud. Thud. The butt end of the staff connected with one chest or stomach before moving on to the next. Four thuds and it was over, the boys sprawled on the ground, howling in agony.

Then the stranger quickly turned to the older boy and the girl on the ground.

Crack!

The sharp blow on the arm cracked a bone, and the youth rolled over, screaming with pain. He looked up, his eyes widening at the sight of an angry man holding a staff. Lurching to his feet, he ran, his arm dangling. The other four boys limped after him, howling or whimpering.

The man then turned his back on the girls and walked to the well. With slow movements, he took one of the buckets, dropped it down, then hauled it up, staring down into the cool water. He lifted the bucket to his lips and drank deeply.

The water tasted sweet and fresh, and a delicious coolness spread through his body. He had not tasted anything so refreshing this past week, possibly in his whole lifetime.

He turned around. The girl now stood on her feet. She seemed calm after her terrible ordeal.

THUD. THUD. THUD. THUD.

He smiled. "I hope you're all right?"

"Yes, I . . ." She paused. Hurriedly adjusting the hood of her burnoose to cover her forehead, she added, "I want to . . ." She lowered her eyes.

The man pursed his lips. She's not as calm as she looks. But before the face retreated into the shadows of her hood, he caught a glimpse of black hair, heavy brows, dark eyes, and sun-browned skin. Not an Egyptian lady, but still pretty in her wild, tawny way.

The other girls now called the sheep, which gathered around them at the sound of their voices. The older girl raised her eyes and tried again to express herself.

"Thank you for. . .what you did. I'll tell my father." She turned and hurried to catch up with the others.

She had not gone ten steps before she stopped, then slowly turned to face him.

"Tell me your name, Egyptian, that I may tell Father."

The man hesitated, then shrugged. "Tell him Moses," he said. "But I'm not an Egyptian. Not anymore."

She didn't wait for an explanation, but turned and hurried after the sheep.

The man named Moses returned to his palm tree and

"THANK YOU FOR...WHAT YOU DID."

sat down wearily. He didn't even know her name. Nor her father's. He shrugged. He'd find out soon enough.

The desert breeze that came with sundown began to blow. He relaxed, wondering when they would come.

That pretty girl had called him an Egyptian. He frowned. One week ago, he had been an Egyptian. But not anymore. Now, he was nobody. *Those boys had called him a dog.* He set his jaw. *They weren't far from the truth.*

With that thought, he closed his eyes. He heard nothing but the whisper of the breeze in the palm trees and the drone of bees.

NOW, HE WAS NOBODY.

"PLEASE COME TO OUR TENT."

2

It was dark when three people finally came for him. Two were young girls whom he had seen earlier that day. The third was a servant-bodyguard. Moses was disappointed that the pretty older girl was not with them.

"Moses. Where are you?" called one of the girls.

Moses pushed himself to his feet, breathing deeply of the cooler air. The evening smelled clean and fresh.

"I'm here."

The two girls ran to him and grasped his hands.

"Please come to our tent. Father wants to meet you."

The girls led him away from the well, down a well-traveled path marked by many hoofprints. They came to a pleasant part of the oasis. The moon had risen, and the stars shone brightly above. Somewhere in the shadows a brook chuckled over rocks. A large black tent stood among several smaller tents. In front of the large tent, a cheerful campfire blazed, its orange light shimmering over a group of people. A man walked toward them, an old man, his gray beard and hair shining softly in the moonlight.

"Moses!" The old man seemed glad to welcome him. He grasped Moses by the shoulders, then hugged him. "I am Jethro, priest of the Kenite Clan of the tribe of Midian. Welcome to my tent. You may stay as long as you wish."

Desert hospitality was generous, especially to weary travelers, but this welcome went beyond the usual greetings of a desert host. Two nights and the day in between was the normal length of stay for a visitor, or a month for a family member. An offer to stay as long as he wished was more than usual for a stranger. Was there some hidden meaning behind such a warm welcome?

"Thank you, Father. I am yours to command." Moses used the term "Father," which showed respect for an older person.

With a hand on his arm, the old man guided Moses toward the blazing campfire. A group of people stood in the shadows just beyond the light of the fire. Moses wondered if one of them was the pretty older girl he had seen this afternoon. He decided to ask.

"The seven girls at the well today. Your daughters?"

"Yes. They are here."

He pointed toward the group of women. One of them stepped forward and bowed low before him. "I am

16

"I AM JETHRO."

Zipporah, Jethro's oldest daughter. Welcome to our home, Moses."

The girl's action was bold and improper. An Egyptian lady might do this, but not a person in this society.

He recognized her immediately: the girl he had met at the well today. The hood of her burnoose left her face in shadows, but he liked the sound of her voice.

"Zipporah," he said slowly. "A lovely name. It has the sound of the desert in it. What does it mean?"

"Little bird."

Then suddenly she seemed to realize how shameless she must appear, for she retreated to the others in the shadows.

Jethro touched his elbow. "Come, Moses. Sit and eat. A table is spread for you."

In front of the campfire, the carpet on the grass showed how things were different here compared to Egypt. Moses seated himself cross-legged on the carpet, remembering just in time to pull off his sandals according to the desert custom.

Moses pointed to a place on the carpet. "What place is this, Father Jethro?"

The old patriarch turned to Moses, smiling. "This place is called Hazeroth. Our oasis is on the western edge

"I AM ZIPPORAH."

of the Sinai Wilderness. We are the children of Midian."

"Midian! But. . .the land of the Midianites is far to the east. Aren't you far from your homeland?"

The old man chuckled. "Not at all, my son. We're Sand Crossers. We go where there is pasture and water. This year there are nine Midian families at Hazeroth. Who knows where we will be next year?" He shrugged. "We are Sand Crossers."

Moses was unfamiliar with this wild area. He had never been here before. He had come this far now only because he was trying to get as far away from Egypt as possible.

The girls then served supper: a pan of good-smelling meat stew and pita, the bread of the desert. Moses was served first, a great honor. What a difference between this desert table and an Egyptian feast, as the women behind him had to wait until the men were finished before they could eat anything. Moses wondered how hungry they were.

Finally the supper was over, and the girls cleared away the dishes and went into the large tent, where they probably ate their own supper at last. Moses and Jethro were left alone by the campfire.

"Moses, my son." Jethro turned his face to him. "I

"WE ARE SAND CROSSERS."

want to thank you again for what you did at the well today."

Moses nodded. "Who are those boys?"

"They are five homeless brothers of the Amalekite tribe."

Moses had learned about the Amalekites in his studies of geography back in Egypt. It was a tribe who lived in many different places in the vast wilderness.

Jethro shook his head sadly. "Since they came here two months ago, they have teased my daughters as they tended the sheep. But this is the first time they tried to attack them."

He seemed sad, but not angry. Then he spoke slowly. "I'm. . .glad you're here. Those boys won't bother our women as long as. . .well, as long as you remain with us."

Was he really trying to say that he wanted Moses to stay for a while. . .for protection? That he needed Moses?

"Don't worry, Father Jethro." Moses grinned. "One of those sons of Amalek will bother no one for quite a while. He accidentally broke his arm this afternoon."

Jethro shook his head slowly. "That was no accident. My daughters described the fight. Where did you learn to fight like that, Moses? Were you a soldier in Egypt?"

Moses nodded. "For a while. That's where I learned

"DON'T WORRY, FATHER JETHRO."

to fight. Those boys are pretty clumsy. . .and untrained."

Jethro nodded. "What else did you do in Egypt?"

Moses hesitated. How much should he tell Jethro? It still hurt to talk about it. But the old man had been so good and kind to him, he felt he should tell the truth. He spoke softly, not wanting the girls in the tent to hear.

"I. . .well, I did a little bit of everything in Egypt. I spent many years in school, learning writing, geography, history, religions, and. . .yes, the military arts."

Jethro was quiet for a moment, studying his visitor. Finally he said, "Who are you, Moses?"

Again Moses hesitated, wondering how much he should tell. Then he shrugged, deciding to tell all.

"I was a prince, Father Jethro. A prince of Egypt."

Jethro nodded. He didn't seem surprised. "Are you a son of the pharaoh?" he asked.

"No, Father." Moses spoke slowly, sadly. "My mother was Princess Asiyeh, daughter of Pharaoh Seti. But. . .she wasn't my real mother. I. . .was adopted."

"Who was your real mother? Do you know?"

"Yes." Moses didn't really want to talk about it, but he owed the old man an explanation. "She was a Josephite. A. . .slave."

"Is that why you fled from Egypt?"

"WHO ARE YOU, MOSES?"

"That's part of the reason. I've left Egypt for good. Now I'm a Sand Crosser. I'd like to stay here as your servant." Jethro was silent for a moment, and Moses listened to the crackling of the fire as the flames grew smaller and became hot coals. Finally, Jethro spoke.

"Moses, let me speak frankly. I believe God sent you to us. You can see how much we need your protection. But there's more. I would like you to be a part of my family."

"Your family?"

"Yes, Moses. I want you among us. . .not as a servant, but as my son."

Moses gasped as he realized what the old man was saying. This was a proposal of marriage! He was offering to Moses one of his daughters as his wife! And his oldest daughter—she would have to be the first to be married!

"Zipporah!"

"Yes, my son. She's attracted to you. I believe she will make you a fine wife."

Moses blinked his eyes. He had hardly expected this. A feeling of excitement gripped him. He was going to marry the pretty little bird and begin his new life. If he couldn't be an Egyptian prince, he could at least be a part of the house of Jethro. And. . .Egypt was far away.

"I BELIEVE GOD SENT YOU TO US."

MOSES AND ZIPPORAH WERE MARRIED.

3

According to Sand Crosser custom, the father made all
the marriage arrangements for a daughter. Usually she
had nothing to say about it. Sometimes this caused
unhappiness if the girl was forced to marry an older man
she didn't like.

Moses was sure this was not the case with Zipporah.
Every time he saw her in the days following, she greeted
him with a warm smile and friendly words. Her eyes,
when she spoke to him, reflected a softness that spoke of
love. Moses hoped his own eyes held the same softness.

A few weeks later, Moses and Zipporah were married in a Sand Crosser ceremony. The other eight
Midianite families encamped at Hazeroth came to the
wedding party. Moses liked the quiet way they had a
party. At Egyptian weddings, everyone would be drunk
and rowdy, with loud music and laughter. Here, the party
was simple but happy. They drank very little wine. The
food was plain: roast lamb, bread, cheese, nuts, and
fruits. These people were serious because they had lived
their lives struggling with the desert. Moses gladly

accepted their ways, having had his fill of the ways of Egypt.

At sundown, Jethro began the wedding ceremony. "Moses." Jethro's priestly voice boomed out over the assembly in front of the black tent. "You are now in my family. My possessions are yours. My daughter is yours. You are one of us. . .and it is good." He paused, looking at Moses. "May God richly bless you, my son. May He give you long life and health. May you serve Him all your life."

Jethro then grasped his daughter's hands.

"Zipporah, my child, I give you to Moses. Go with him. Live with him as long as you live. God bless you, my child."

He then kissed her and placed her hands in Moses' hands. The ceremony completed, the family and guests crowded around the newlyweds with kisses and blessings.

Another Sand Crosser wedding custom was for the bride and groom to spend a whole week together. They did not have to go to the pasture to watch the sheep; instead they had time to get to know each other. They would be living together as close companions for the rest of their lives. Now was the time to tell each other everything. Moses, however, hesitated to tell her about his life

"ZIPPORAH, MY CHILD, I GIVE YOU TO MOSES."

in Egypt. But Zipporah was curious. She asked a very personal question.

"Moses, my love." She stroked his face. "Tell me about your past. Your Egyptian mother. Why you left Egypt so abruptly. What made you so unhappy."

Moses knew he would have to tell her. There could be no secrets between them. Then, with a sigh of relief, he realized that he wanted to tell her. For several weeks, this had been bothering him, and he needed to talk about it to someone. They were so close, so loving. The two were one. Nothing—no secrets—must come between them.

And so he told her, leaving out nothing. He told of his mother, the princess Asiyah, daughter of Pharaoh Seti. He told her of his Egyptian childhood, his schooling, his military training, his preparation for a position in government. He told about his search for religion, his study of the Egyptian gods and goddesses, and how he didn't like any of them. He talked about all this with a sadness and a longing that seemed to impress Zipporah.

"You love Egypt, don't you?"

Moses turned his head away. "I was an Egyptian. But not now. I'm a Sand Crosser. And I can never go back."

"Why not, Moses? Why can't you return?"

"YOU LOVE EGYPT, DON'T YOU?"

Moses touched her hand. "Little bird, I can't. I killed an Egyptian and now I'm a fugitive from justice."

"Who did you kill that makes you a desperate criminal?"

He shrugged. "Just a taskmaster. A slave overseer."

"Is that all? But you're an Egyptian prince."

Moses turned his head away. When he spoke, his voice was soft. "But. . .there's more. I can't go back."

Zipporah frowned. "More, Moses? Tell me. What causes your suffering?"

Moses paused, wondering how to say it.

"Yes, my love. You should know the truth. I learned it myself only a few weeks ago, just before I left Egypt."

"Tell me your secret, Moses. Please."

He sighed. "I'm not an Egyptian prince. I'm not even an Egyptian. I'm a Josephite slave."

Zipporah shook her head. "I don't understand, my love. You said your mother was the Princess As . . .Asiy. . .whatever her name is. How can you be a slave?"

"I was adopted. My true parents were Josephites from the Upper Delta."

"Is that so terrible?"

He nodded. He spoke so softly she had to bend a

34

"I WAS ADOPTED."

little closer to hear him. "When I was young, I was an Egyptian prince, with an exciting future. Then suddenly, I was a slave. A murderer. A fugitive. A nobody."

"How did you find out? Did your mother tell you?"

"Not at first." Moses looked in her eyes. "I found out by accident. One day I was in the Upper Delta watching the Josephites making their straw bricks for the pharaoh's city. I came upon an Egyptian taskmaster. . . beating a slave."

"Poor man!"

"The man was dead. The Egyptian had beaten him to death. He continued to hit the dead body with his whip, looking as though he enjoyed it."

"How awful!"

"That was what I thought at the time. In fact, I . . .well, I went a little crazy. I killed the taskmaster."

"You killed him? But how—"

"It was nothing. To someone trained to fight the way I had been, it was easy. And. . .he deserved to die."

"Nobody deserves to die, Moses. God gives life. Only He can take it."

Moses smiled. "You're thinking like a Sand Crosser, my love. Remember, I was trained to think like an Egyptian."

"I KILLED THE TASKMASTER."

"What did you do then?"

"Nobody was around, so I buried the Egyptian in the sand. Then I carried the dead Josephite to some nearby workers, who promised to take the body to the man's family."

"But. . .what did this have to do with your finding out about being a Josephite? Did they tell you then?"

"No. The next day, I came across two Josephites in the field. They were arguing. I offered to settle their dispute."

"What happened?"

"They turned on me angrily. One of them said, 'What'll you do, kill us like you killed that Egyptian yesterday?'"

"Oh, Moses! How did he know?"

"I don't know. But if he knew, then everybody knew."

"But you're an Egyptian prince. You had nothing to fear."

"That's what I thought, too. But then they told me."

"What did they tell you?"

"That I was one of them." Moses sighed. "It seems every Josephite in the Upper Delta knew all about me."

"Did you believe them?"

"THEY TURNED ON ME ANGRILY."

"No. But it bothered me, and so I went directly to my mother and demanded the truth. And she told me."

"Told you what?"

"That she had found me in a small reed basket floating in the Great River. She knew immediately that I was one of those slaves. And she knew that Josephite boy babies were being murdered in the Upper Delta."

"Then your Josephite mother saved your life by putting you into the river to be found by the princess!"

"Yes, I suppose she did. My Egyptian mother took me in, knowing exactly who I was. She kept the secret. She told everyone she was my natural mother."

"But. . .how did she explain who your father was?"

Moses shrugged. "She didn't. This was Egypt, and she was a princess. She didn't have to explain to anybody."

"Oh. That world is so different from ours."

Moses stared at her. "Yes. So. . .now I'm a Sand Crosser. By birth, by marriage, and by the sand between my toes."

Zipporah reached out and grasped his hand. "Moses, my love. Please don't be bitter. We will give you. . .love."

Moses' arm went around her and drew her close. "You're right, little bird. It'll take time, but already I've

"SHE FOUND ME IN A SMALL REED BASKET."

found some of that peace. And best of all, I've found love."

Zipporah looked directly into his eyes, and he saw there softness and tenderness. He smiled. Yes. He had found love.

"BEST OF ALL, I'VE FOUND LOVE."

MOSES BECAME A SHEPHERD.

4

In the months that followed the wedding week, Moses became a shepherd. As an Egyptian prince, he had learned many things, but never how to take care of a flock of sheep.

Jethro himself was his teacher. Moses suspected that Jethro really wanted to introduce his son-in-law to his God. But Moses had no objection. He listened carefully to everything Jethro told him about his God.

"Already I like your God," Moses told him one day. "I like Him because you are so sincere, not like the priests I knew in Egypt. Tell me your God's name, Father. I have studied about all the gods. Perhaps I know about Him already."

"We don't know His name, Moses. He has never revealed it to us, not even to our ancestor Abraham. My father roamed these deserts all his life, asking God His name, but he was never told. God hasn't yet chosen the man to whom He shall reveal it."

All his life, Moses had been searching for a god he could accept, but had never found one in all the gods of

Egypt. He wanted to believe in some god. Maybe. . . maybe Jethro's God.

"Father," he said, his voice hushed. "You must teach me. I would like to know more about your God."

Jethro nodded. "There's much to tell, my son."

"I want you to instruct me, Father Jethro. But I must warn you, I'm not a religious person."

Jethro smiled. "I don't think that's true, Moses. I've known you briefly. And yet I know you. You're a lot like me. . .a very religious man. Will you fight it, Moses? Or will you let God touch your life and give it meaning?"

"Father, you're wrong. I'd like to be religious, but I can't. I may be a Josephite by birth, but by education, by the way I think, by religious training, I'm an Egyptian. I have a scientific turn of mind. I could never be religious."

Jethro shook his head. "There are two kinds of men who cross the sand, my son. One walks with his head down. He sees the desert. The other walks with his head up. He sees God."

Jethro's statement made Moses remember a lesson from his childhood. One of Moses' teachers had said something like it once. Something about two kinds of minds. One was educated, scientific, looking for explanations in nature and science. The other was religious,

"WILL YOU LET GOD TOUCH YOUR LIFE?"

believing that everything can be explained by believing in God. One mind was intellectual; the other. . .superstitious. Moses had always believed that all religious people were merely superstitious.

"In all honesty, Father, I walk with my head down, seeing reality. I am not a religious person."

"Perhaps." Jethro shrugged, giving Moses the impression he didn't believe what Moses said about not being religious. "But someday. . .someday. . .God will touch your life, and you will never be the same. When it happens, you will know."

Moses did not want to be disrespectful, but he could not resist an impudent grin. "It shall be as you say, Father. When your God tells me His name, then I will look up. Until then, I will walk with my head down."

Jethro frowned, evidently not liking Moses' flippancy. He sighed. "We'll see, my son."

Jethro's teachings to Moses in the weeks that followed contained two kinds of lessons. One was to explain the mysteries of the desert. The other was to teach him about God. Moses marveled at how cleverly Jethro combined the two.

The oasis at Hazeroth was large enough for the nine Midianite families and more, including the five Amalekite

"WHEN YOUR GOD TELLS ME HIS NAME..."

brothers. But they seldom saw their enemies. Nevertheless, Moses stayed close to the family. When they moved their flocks from one pasture to another, seeking fresh grass, Moses remained nearby. And as they traveled, Jethro continued to teach Moses.

"I want to learn the desert's secrets, Father. Tell me more, Father Jethro," Moses would say.

"The desert has only one secret, Moses," Jethro would answer. "You must trust God. He will take care of you."

"Spoken like a Sand Crosser, Father. I still want to know the desert's secrets."

Jethro laughed. "Spoken like an Egyptian, Moses. You must stop searching for scientific explanations. You must see God at work in His world."

"But I see no God at work in the desert, Father. I see only the desert, with its great mysteries. I hope I'm not offending you."

"Honesty is not offensive, Moses. Only disrespect. You're new here among us. When you've lived in the desert for a time, our ways will be your ways and our God your God."

"Maybe so, Father." Again Moses hesitated. But Jethro had said that honesty was not offensive, and so he

"THE DESERT HAS ONLY ONE SECRET, MOSES."

continued. "All my life I have been taught by Egyptians. It won't be easy to become a Sand Crosser in my thinking."

Jethro spoke softly. "You probably won't, my son, until God Himself speaks to you. In fact, I believe you might be the one to whom God has chosen to reveal His name. We'll see."

The days passed swiftly and blended into weeks, which merged with the months and entwined with the years. Moses found happiness as a shepherd among the Sand Crossers. Egypt was far away, a vague memory, another world.

The family moved from one oasis to another. They were Sand Crossers, whose sheep constantly needed fresh pasturage.

At first, Zipporah went with him as he took a flock out to distant pastures. Jethro would not let them be separated. She was safe under the protection of his military skill and had nothing to fear from the Amalekite boys—now grown to manhood—who had bothered her at Hazeroth. Occasionally they saw them during their wanderings with the sheep, but the young men kept their distance when they saw Moses.

One day Zipporah stayed in the camp. She told

THE YOUNG MEN KEPT THEIR DISTANCE.

Moses, "I will soon have another little bird to care for." Moses was delighted. He would have a child! A boy, he hoped.

Among the Sand Crossers—far more so than in Egypt—the chief function of a wife was to produce sons so that the family name could be carried on. Family life was important to them. Moses looked forward to holding his son in his arms.

And so Zipporah stayed in camp, and Moses resumed his shepherding with his father and teacher, Jethro.

Many were the lessons of the desert Moses learned from Jethro. They were always intertwined with lessons about God. What Jethro said made sense, not to an Egyptian, but to a Sand Crosser. And Moses was gradually becoming a Sand Crosser. Now. . .if only this mysterious God would speak to him. . . .

Moses shook his head in wonderment. Maybe he was beginning to walk the desert now with his head up . . .seeing God!

MOSES SHOOK HIS HEAD IN WONDERMENT.

"MY SON!"

5

"My son!"

Moses spoke the words softly, as he held the new-born infant in his hands. Moses felt the thrill of seeing a newly created life as he gazed down at the small squalling baby. He wondered if all parents in every age felt this excitement at holding a new life.

Jethro, too, was thrilled. He had no sons. His new grandson would be his heir.

"Have you named your son yet?" asked Jethro.

Moses nodded. "He shall be called Gershom."

The name came from root words in Sand Crosser language, meaning "traveler" and "here in this place."

Jethro pulled his gray beard thoughtfully. "Gershom. Do you still consider yourself a stranger in this place?"

"No, Jethro." Moses smiled. "A traveler. But not a stranger. Here I will stay for as long as I live. And my son will remain here after I'm gone. This is my home."

"I hope so," replied Jethro. "But we never know what God has in mind for our future."

Five years passed quickly and happily. One morning, as Moses, Zipporah, and Jethro laughed and played with Gershom, Moses said to Jethro, "I've been here several years now, and still your God hasn't spoken to me. Why do you think that is?"

"But He has spoken to you, my son." The old man ran his fingers through his beard. "Look at your son. Is that not God speaking to you?"

Moses nodded. "Yes. But—forgive me, Father—I'm still not sure. How desperately I want to have a faith like yours."

The old man nodded. "I know you do, Moses. And I have prayed for God to reveal Himself to you. I believe the answer to that prayer will come any day now."

"I hope so." Moses shook his head sadly. "Do you think if I climb that mountain, God will speak to me?"

Jethro was silent for a moment. Finally he said, "It may be so. God is everywhere, but sometimes He reveals Himself in high, lonely places. I climbed that mountain once, and I felt closer to God there than any other time in my life."

The mountain they were talking about was the one where they were encamped at this time. Moses was impressed by it.

"SOMETIMES HE REVEALS HIMSELF
IN HIGH LONELY PLACES."

In Moses' geography lessons back in Egypt, he had learned that the mountain was called "Sinai" by the Egyptians. It was named for Sin, the moon goddess. But Jethro did not like to use the name because of the false goddess it was named for, and so he called it "Horeb." The name was appropriate, meaning "wild." Moses looked up at its towering height. He thought it looked very wild.

"Why don't I climb it today?" he said to Jethro. "If God is ever going to speak to me, maybe this is the time."

Just then one of Jethro's servants strode into the campsite and came directly to the carpet in front of Jethro's tent, where Jethro and Moses were playing with Gershom.

"Is something wrong?" asked Moses.

"No. But I came to tell you we have a visitor."

"Who is he?"

"His name is Aaron. He's from Egypt. And all he would tell us is that he's looking for you."

"For me?"

"Yes, Moses, for you."

"Aaron." Moses ran his fingers through his beard. "I know of no one by that name. Is he an Egyptian?"

"No, Moses. He claims to be an Israelite."

"HIS NAME IS AARON. HE'S LOOKING FOR YOU."

"What's an Israelite?"

"I don't know. Perhaps an Egyptian clan. But you should ask him these questions yourself. He's on his way and should be here any minute now."

Another servant came into camp just then with their visitor. When Zipporah saw the stranger, she knew she had work to do to prepare a meal for the guest, so she took Gershom and left, leaving the men to welcome their visitor. They stood on the carpet outside Jethro's tent and greeted the stranger warmly.

Moses looked him over carefully. His long hair and beard made it clear that he was not an Egyptian. Egyptians were smooth-shaven.

"Moses!" The stranger—Aaron—stepped forward. Tears streamed down his cheeks onto his beard. "Moses! My brother!"

"I'm not your brother," he said.

Moses invited him to sit on the carpet, and Aaron, remembering his manners, pulled off his dusty sandals before stepping on the carpet. He sat down.

Moses listened, astonished, as Aaron told him that they were indeed blood brothers, who shared the same parents. He had come from Goshen, which Moses called the Upper Delta, and his people were Israelites.

"MOSES! MY BROTHER!"

"Don't you mean Josephites?"

"No, Israelites." Aaron pulled his matted beard. "The Egyptians call us Josephites. But Joseph was not our main ancestor. Israel was."

"But. . .how do you know who I am?"

"Every Israelite knows who you are. We have known ever since our mother Jochabed put you in an ark of reeds and set you adrift in the Great River. We followed your growth into young manhood. When you left abruptly to go to the desert, we knew it was God's will."

"What God is that?"

Aaron raised his eyebrows in surprise. "You don't know? Hasn't He spoken to you yet? Well, we don't know His name, but He is the God of our ancestors, Abraham, Isaac, and Jacob. I can hardly believe you don't know Him."

The first named ancestor caught Jethro's attention. "Abraham? Do we have a common ancestor?"

"It looks like it, Father Jethro," said Moses.

Jethro smiled. "Then you are thrice welcome here. Not only are you a stranger in my tent, but you are also a distant relative—and a fellow believer in God. Welcome, my friend."

Aaron nodded his thanks, then turned to Moses.

"BUT...HOW DO YOU KNOW WHO I AM?"

"I've come into the desert seeking you, my brother. Fo
several months I have wandered in the wilderness look
ing for you. Through God's guidance I have come to you
at last!"

"But why?"

Aaron looked steadily into Moses' eyes. "You mus
come back to Egypt, Moses. It is time. It is God's will.'

His words gave Moses an uneasy feeling. Somehow
deep within him, he had known that this would happen
someday.

"What do you mean?"

"We've always known God's hand was on you in a
special way. It was God who brought the ark of reeds to
the feet of Princess Asiyah. Because God was with you,
you were given an Egyptian education, preparing you to
be our leader. Then He led you into the desert so that you
could become a religious man and follow the ways of
God. Now the time has come for you to do the job God
has planned for you."

He paused. Moses had a deep feeling that important
events were happening, that his life was being led by
powers beyond his control.

Aaron continued. "It is God's will, Brother. Our
burdens are too heavy. When our ancestor Israel led us

"YOU MUST COME BACK TO EGYPT, MOSES."

down into Egypt, he settled us in Goshen, a good and pleasant land. But it is pleasant no more. It is bitter, for we are slaves. Even now, Pharaoh Ramses is increasing our—"

"Ramses!" Moses exclaimed. "But. . .Pharaoh Seti—"

"He's dead. His son Ramses sits on the throne. And his taskmasters grow more cruel. The time has come for us to leave, to go to the land our God promised us."

"If Ramses is pharaoh, he'll never let you go."

Aaron spoke firmly. "He'll let us go, Brother. It's God's will, and God is more powerful than a pharaoh of Egypt."

Again Moses felt that something important was happening. And he was a part of it. What Aaron said next made him sure.

"All we need now is a leader, one through whom God speaks. You, Moses. The time has come."

Moses shook his head. He didn't want to believe this. Those people weren't his people. He hadn't been called by a God to lead slaves. Nonsense. Ridiculous. Impossible.

But he could not escape the feeling that he had to do it. He had to. There was no escape. And it was a burden.

"GOD IS MORE POWERFUL THAN A PHARAOH OF EGYPT."

A burden he didn't want.

He had found peace here among the Sand Crossers. He had married and had a son, an heir. They needed him. And he needed them. He wanted to live out his life in peace, to study the mysteries of the desert, to search for this God who both Jethro and Aaron knew. He wanted to die here. He was now and forever a Sand Crosser, a child of the desert.

The scene around him seemed like a frozen picture. They sat with their visitor on the carpet outside the big tent. He looked at the familiar faces of his family. Then he looked up. Above them towered that mountain.

The mountain!

Suddenly he felt the need to climb the mountain, to seek its peace, to get away from these people. Maybe he would meet God up there. If so, perhaps this God would tell him what to do—and how to find peace of mind. He could go there, now, to lift the burden that weighed so heavily on him.

He stood up. Aaron rose also. Moses grasped his shoulder.

"Stay here, Aaron. Enjoy the hospitality of Jethro's tent. I'll be away for a day or two. Wait for me here."

Aaron nodded. He peered thoughtfully into Moses'

"STAY HERE, AARON."

face, perhaps sensing the deep struggle in his brother.

Moses nodded also, understanding his brother's pain and weariness. Not the weariness of the long journey in the desert that he had just completed. But another pain, a weariness Moses could only guess at. It was the burden that his people carried.

Moses spoke briefly to Jethro, who understood. He said nothing, but grasped Moses' shoulders in silent approval.

No more words were spoken as Moses turned and walked away. The mountain was waiting for him.

MOSES TURNED AND WALKED AWAY.

THE LANDSCAPE WAS WILD AND CRAGGY.

6

Moses began immediately, eager for his adventure. He filled his waterbag and packed some bread, then started out. It was still morning, and he shouldn't take long to climb. He had already picked out his route.

Climbing the mountain proved easy for someone like Moses, in good physical condition. Soon he lost sight of the camp as the cleft he followed led him around boulders and through crannies and across rock slides. The time-tumbled landscape was wild and craggy, with a haunting beauty that was both pleasant and scary. It began as an easy climb in the fresh coolness of the morning, but before long the burning heat of the day scorched the barren rock face.

By noon he had reached the top.

Up here, he felt different. Something was weird about it. He shivered, but not from cold.

What was this eerie feeling that possessed him, this strange sensation that made him feel so unsettled? His Egyptian-trained mind struggled to gain mastery over the feelings that gripped him.

What was it he felt? What made him feel this way? Was it the gentle wind that ruffled his hair and beard? Was it the beauty of the distant landscape? No. It was something else. What?

The silence?

Yes. The silence. The relentless, enveloping silence. *How strange,* he thought, *that we who live in a world of constant noise have never known the awesome experience of total silence.* He didn't just hear the silence; he felt it.

But there was something more. Something was beyond the silence that he couldn't understand. It almost seemed someone else was up here on the mountain with him. Some strange, unseen Presence. What was it?

He took a deep breath and grinned. Get hold of yourself, Moses. Think like an Egyptian. Appreciate the moment, but don't be swallowed up in it. Look at it. Analyze it. Understand it. And enjoy it. But don't go looking for any weird, unseen Presence.

While he was here, alone, in the silence of the mountain, he might as well think about what Aaron had just told him.

Prince Ramses. Pharaoh Ramses now. What kind of a ruler would he make? This tall, handsome youth, with his energy and ambition—would the people of Egypt

THE RELENTLESS, ENVELOPING SILENCE.

like him as pharaoh? It didn't matter. Ramses would force himself on them and cruelly put down anyone who objected.

And the Josephite slaves? Would they be any better off under this new pharaoh? No, Moses was sure. Aaron had brought him word that his people suffered. They felt the urgent need to escape their slavery, to get away to live a life of their own. All they needed now was a leader.

A leader. Moses. There it was again, that sense of important things happening. But something—he didn't know what—seemed to be driving him.

What was it that made him feel that way? He looked up into the sky, as though there he could find an answer. But nothing was there.

The sun approached the western horizon. What had happened to the day? Time seemed to blur in this unreal landscape. The golden rays of the setting sun awakened colors in the distance, picking out the blues and reds of the far mountains. Shadows crept across the plain. Distant scenes faded as he watched, the colors changing. The world was growing dark, as the day came to an end.

Suddenly, the darkness was there, and Moses stood alone, not moving, alert, listening to the voice of the mountain.

SHADOWS CREPT ACROSS THE PLAIN.

The voice of the mountain thundered in its silence. And once again he felt that strange sensation that someone else—a Presence—was there with him.

The night became darker. Something was happening to the stars; they were fading out. It was so dark, he couldn't see anything. He felt alone. Even the mountain was gone, cutting him off from everything and everybody. He seemed to be the only one left in an empty universe. A cold, thick cloud surrounded him, leaving him alone. There was nothing. . .nothing but darkness, emptiness, loneliness.

And yet. . .and yet. . .he wasn't alone. Again he had that scary feeling that someone else was on the mountain with him.

As he stood there in the night, suddenly the morning ambushed him. What had happened to the night? Time passed so quickly on the mountain.

The morning seeped in, calmly and with great dignity. Unlike the sunset, he saw no shafts of golden rays from the sun. He couldn't see the sun at all. Something had changed in the night; a totally new world had been created.

Moses gasped at what he saw.

The mountain stood alone in the universe. The summit

MOSES GASPED AT WHAT HE SAW.

on which he stood thrust itself above a thick layer of clouds that stretched as far as he could see. And that was all he could see. He was on a little island in a sea of clouds, and there was nothing else in the whole universe.

No, that wasn't all. There was definitely something else. Or rather. . .someone. He was not alone up here.

He looked around, expecting to see someone. But there was no one, nothing but the rocks, the clouds. . .and a bush.

That bush—it seemed to burn. Yes! It was burning! But how could that be? No lightning had struck. The bush couldn't be burning. But it was. He watched it, a flickering mass of colors. Orange blended into pink, then brown, then white, then yellow, then orange again. The branches showed dark through the flames. To Moses' numbed mind, it looked as though the bush burned but was not being burned up.

He shook himself to get rid of the illusion. This is a shaft of sunlight, he told himself. Nothing more. It's something that has a very natural explanation.

But he knew it wasn't. Something else was here. Something big. Something beyond his experience.

THAT BUSH—IT SEEMED TO BURN.

THE PRESENCE SURROUNDING HIM WAS SO STRONG.

7

Then suddenly, he knew. In a moment of clarity, he recognized what made this moment.

God.

The Presence surrounding him was so strong, so vivid, it seemed to grip him—more real in that moment than the burnoose around his shoulders and the sandals on his feet. He could not mistake this Presence. It was here.

Almost without thinking, he took off his sandals—an act of politeness among the Sand Crossers. He was in God's house now. It was as if the Presence had spoken to him, telling him to take off his shoes.

He thought he heard—no, he heard!—a Voice. The Voice was calling him.

Moses! Moses!

He stood before a living God.

He remembered what Aaron had said yesterday: ". . .the God of your fathers, Abraham, Isaac, and Jacob. . ." This was the God in whose presence he stood, who was speaking to him now.

And Moses was scared. He cringed before the Presence. His arms wrapped themselves around his face. He blotted out the vision of the Presence, but he could not erase it from his mind.

The Presence was there, and the Voice spoke in the silence. *I am God* it seemed to say. *I am God. I am. I AM. I AM.* The beat of these two syllables inside his mind was insistent and clear. *Yah-weh! I am! Yah-weh! I am! YAH-WEH! I AM!*

He gasped. What he heard stunned him. This was. . . the name of God! He knew the name of God!

Suddenly the Presence seemed to calm him. He no longer had that feeling of terror. It was a friendly Presence. . . .It had told him Its name. He could walk with this Presence as a close friend because Yahweh, the eternal I AM, had given him His name!

Slowly he dropped his arms and looked again. The bush still flamed, although it still didn't burn. The Presence was still there. But the fear had vanished. Instead, there was peace. At last, God was with him!

Moses listened as the Voice continued to speak. He listened carefully because Yahweh was giving him instructions. He was to go back to Egypt, to speak to the pharaoh, and demand that God's people—Israel—be

THE PRESENCE WAS THERE.

released from slavery so they could go to their promised land.

As Moses listened, his peaceful feeling began to disappear. "What if the people don't believe me?" he said out loud. "What if they won't listen?" All his logical, scientific training rose up inside of him, telling him this plan was foolish, that none of it made sense. *Maybe I've taken leave of my senses,* his thoughts whispered. *Maybe my mind is playing tricks on me and none of this is real.* After all, that was the most logical explanation for the Voice and the burning bush.

What do you have in your hand? the Voice asked.

The question was so unexpected that Moses was startled. He looked at his hand. "It's just my staff." His fingers curled tighter around the sturdy stick. He had found it years ago when he'd been a very young man, exploring the banks of the Great River. It was the one thing he'd brought with him when he fled Egypt, and by now he'd been depending on the staff's support for so many years that the gnarled stick seemed a part of him.

Throw it on the ground, commanded the Voice.

But I don't want to, Moses thought. *Why should I? This makes no sense.*

Throw it down, the Voice insisted quietly.

THROW IT DOWN, THE VOICE INSISTED.

Reluctantly, Moses let the staff drop onto the rocky ground. And then he sucked in his breath and his muscles froze.

The staff's twisted, silvery wood was changing before his eyes. It shifted, straightened, darkened, and then it writhed like a live thing. A red forked tongue flickered from one end and a pointed tail twitched on the other.

"My staff. . ." Moses said stupidly, staring at the snake.

Pick it up by the tail. The Voice sounded like It might be amused.

Moses bent over. His hand hovered a moment over the long snake. He saw the bright slit eyes and the scaly pattern that rippled restlessly. *A trick of my mind,* he thought desperately. His fingers closed around the snake's tail; he felt the scales and the fierce jerk of muscles. It's real.

And then suddenly the snake was stiff in his hand, once more a dead stick. He stared at it suspiciously, then cautiously tested his weight on it. It held him just as it always had—but he knew he would never again feel the same about it.

If the people don't believe you, said the Voice, *I think*

"MY STAFF..."

something like that should convince them.

"A trick?" whispered Moses.

A sign, corrected the Voice.

Moses ran his hand up and down the staff. If Yahweh could turn his old, dead stick into a live, wild creature, then surely He could do anything. Moses bowed his head, accepting Yahweh's will.

The Voice was silent now. Moses lifted his head and slowly began to approach the burning shrub. Before his eyes the flame disappeared. The bush became a bush again.

The moment was gone, but it would never be forgotten. He knew that the awesome feeling of the Presence would be with him forever. God had touched his life and would always be there. And He was good.

He knew what he must do, because the Presence in the burning bush had somehow told him. He would go to those people, the Josephites—no, the Israelites. He would be one of them and be their leader. Then he would stand before Pharaoh Ramses and demand their release from slavery.

Could it be done? Knowing what he knew about Ramses, would Ramses let them go? Then suddenly Moses felt very confident. Yes! Of course it could be

GOD HAD TOUCHED HIS LIFE.

done. God was real, alive. He could make dead wood come alive. Nobody—not even the pharaoh of Egypt—could stand before Yahweh, the living God. The Presence Moses sensed on this mountain was greater than the power of a pharaoh.

But could Moses do it? Could he stand before the people of Israel and be their leader? He couldn't even speak their language well. Doubt touched him again—but what a flimsy excuse, he realized. He remembered a part of the instructions God had given him. Aaron would stand beside him and do most of the talking to his people. Together they would overcome the language problem. The only important thing was that God was with them.

God was with them! That was all that mattered. This living Presence, so real to him on the mountain, would go with him to Egypt. God would lead His people out of Egypt, away from the pharaoh, the slavery, the meaninglessness, to a new life and a new land. They would be the people of Yahweh. All Moses had to do was tell them the name of God.

The name! God had given him a name to tell them!

He recalled his discussion with Jethro about the name of God. Jethro did not know it. Neither did Aaron. All they knew was to call Him "God," but that wasn't

GOD HAD GIVEN HIM A NAME.

His name. If their ancestor Abraham knew it, it was not remembered.

And the name of God was important. To an Egyptian, a name was not important, just something to call a person. But Moses was a Sand Crosser now, and to them a name told what the person really was like.

Yahweh. I am. What a great name! It meant so many things. It meant that God was real. It meant He was now, not a God of the past or present. In Yahweh's Presence, past and present no longer existed, only the forever now.

Nobody else knew this name. Only Moses and his people. They were more than just Israel. They were the chosen people of God.

Moses lifted his head, and his chest heaved. Even without the burning bush, the Presence was still there.

The cloud cover began to clear as sunlight broke through and flooded the mountaintop with friendly sunshine. The bush was nothing more than a bush, but the Presence was still there.

Moses knew the Presence would always be there. Wherever he went, to Egypt, to wander in this wilderness, or to a new land, God would be with him. For He was the eternal I AM.

THE PRESENCE WAS STILL THERE.

On the third day, Moses came down from the mountain.

Aaron and Jethro stood at the edge of the camp, waiting for him. As he came near, after the silence of the mountain, little sounds seemed extremely loud.

"Come, my friends." Moses spoke softly, calmly. "Let's go into the big tent. I have much to tell you."

The shadows inside the tent provided a welcome coolness both from the desert heat and the bright sunlight. The familiar odors of old skin and dried food contrasted sharply with the clean, fresh scent of the mountaintop. The carpet on which he sat was comfortable, and his bare feet nestled in its softness. Moses relaxed and told his story.

"God spoke to me on the mountain."

On his way down, he had carefully thought out how he would tell his story. Not as an Egyptian would: filled with a lot of scientific explanations for everything that happened. He told them the Sand Crosser way.

"God spoke to me in a burning bush. But the bush was not consumed by the flames. As I approached, God called me from the bush, saying, 'Moses! Moses!'"

As Moses continued to describe his experience on the mountain, he was startled to discover that in his own

"GOD SPOKE TO ME ON THE MOUNTAIN."

thinking he was now as much a Sand Crosser as an Egyptian. He had really heard God speaking to him.

The faces of the two men in the dim shadows of the tent showed belief. Nothing like that had ever happened to them, but they both knew it had happened to Moses. An Egyptian would have told Moses he was crazy, he had been hearing things, he was superstitious. But Aaron and Jethro were not Egyptians; God could speak to Moses if He wanted to. Moses spoke the truth, and they accepted it through the eyes of faith.

Moses' story was long, and he had to repeat parts of it in the accent of the Israelites for Aaron's benefit. Aaron's reaction moved him. With a little cry, he grasped Moses' hand and kissed it. Tears dropped on Moses' palm.

Moses understood how Aaron felt. His people had been suffering for a long time now, longing for deliverance, desperately needing a leader. God's all-powerful hand had wisely led them to this moment in time. He had delivered Moses as a baby to the Princess Asiyeh, that he might have an Egyptian education. He had led Moses to the wilderness to prepare for the leadership to come. And now God had spoken to Moses on the mountain. The moment was important. The time had come.

Moses turned to Jethro. "With your permission,

THE TIME HAD COME.

Father, I'll go to Egypt now to be with my people. It's God's will."

Jethro nodded, but his voice held sorrow. "Go with my blessing, my son."

"GO WITH MY BLESSING, MY SON."

"I'M GOING TO HAVE ANOTHER BABY."

8

The hardest part about leaving was saying good-bye to his family. Zipporah held him tightly.

"Don't go, my love," she whispered. "I'm going to have another baby. I need you."

Moses gasped. What a terrible time to leave! But he must. It was Yahweh's will.

"I'll be back as soon as I can," said Moses. "I'll miss you."

When he said good-bye to Gershom, the boy asked, "Can I come with you, Father? Please?"

"No," replied Moses. "I wish you could. But it's too dangerous. Don't worry. I'll be back as soon as I can."

Moses' thoughts as he traveled were disturbing. How different he was from the man who had left Egypt so many years ago! Then he had been alone, an Egyptian, with no other thought in his mind than to escape from Egypt. He had no God to believe in. At first he was an Egyptian, then a Sand Crosser. Now he was an Israelite, who believed in God, to whom God had spoken and had given him a life work.

Moses and Aaron crossed the Sinai wilderness and came to the Red Sea. They traveled north, then, until they came to the Bitter Lakes, then across the narrow strip of land between the Great Bitter Lake and the Lesser Bitter Lake. They followed the Sea of Reeds north toward the Upper Delta, or Goshen, as Aaron called it.

Goshen seemed well populated. Sheep grazed on the fertile countryside. Small brick and mud houses were scattered across the plain, and gardens abounded. Moses marveled, as he had done when he lived here, that these people—who were slaves and really owned nothing—would take such good care of the property they lived on, which belonged not to them but to the pharaoh.

He turned to Aaron. "Why do they do it, Brother? Why tend the sheep, cultivate gardens, keep the houses so clean and neat? None of it belongs to them. What's the point?"

Aaron shrugged. "It's God's will," he answered.

They came to a substantial house with a well-kept garden. "That's our home," said Aaron. "Our mother should be inside."

Moses began to feel a strange uneasiness when he saw his real mother's home. Jochabed. He only vaguely

SHEEP GRAZED ON THE FERTILE COUNTRYSIDE.

remembered her serving in his adopted mother's house. When she left, he was only four, and he had never known that she was his real mother. He dimly recalled the man Amram—his father—and the girl Miriam—his sister—and Aaron not at all.

He embraced his mother tenderly and kissed her cheek. The plow of time had furrowed her skin. Her gray hair was neatly bound in back of her head. Yet she had a bounce in her step and a lilt in her voice that made her seem younger.

Aaron went out to the pasture to find Amram and Miriam, leaving Moses to a somewhat awkward time with his mother.

Moses stroked his beard thoughtfully. In his mother's eyes, he had changed considerably. Now, he was a Sand Crosser, bearded, with desert-lined face and travel-stained burnoose. No doubt Jochabed remembered him as a little boy.

They didn't have long to wait before Aaron came in with Amram and Miriam. Amram's greeting was tender. Moses embraced and kissed his father, noting his wrinkled, brown-spotted skin and stringy white hair and beard. He seemed older than Jochabed, both in years and health.

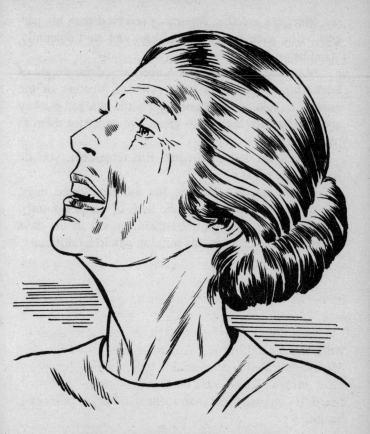

IN HIS MOTHER'S EYES, HE HAD CHANGED.

Miriam's greeting was more reserved than his parents'. She gave him a formal kiss and said solemnly, "God be with you, Moses."

Moses soon learned that Aaron carried the weight of leadership in Israel. "I have called a meeting of the elders," he told Moses. "Fortunately the pharaoh is away and our burdens are not so great. I'm eager for them to meet you."

Moses nodded. "All right. But remember, you do most of the talking."

Aaron agreed. And so, for the next three days, Moses became absorbed in the lives of his new family. Moses knew he would need their support in the days ahead because he knew his mission would be difficult.

MIRIAM'S GREETING WAS MORE RESERVED.

MOSES AND AARON STRODE BOLDLY.

9

Moses met with the elders, and Aaron told them about their experience in the wilderness. They were impressed and overjoyed when Moses told them that God had revealed His name: Yahweh. Knowing God's name made them feel very close to Him.

The next day Moses and Aaron went to work as slaves. Their job was making bricks. The Israelites were building the city of Raamses, named for Pharaoh Ramses. The extra letter in the name meant a city, not a person. When they heard that Ramses had returned to Egypt, Moses and Aaron went to see him.

Moses and Aaron strode boldly into the great audience hall of the palace. Their long hair and beards, their flowing desert robes, their shepherds' staffs were in sharp contrast to the clean-shaven, linen-clothed Egyptians.

Although not the first time Moses had been in the presence of a pharaoh, the meeting was nevertheless impressive. The scene was awesome to him; he couldn't imagine the impact upon Aaron.

The room was large, marble-solid, with stately pillars. The walls were brown, blue, pink, and green, inlaid with precious gems, with pictures of gods and goddesses in bas-relief. At the center of the room sat the pharaoh, drawing attention. His throne was a golden chair on a marble platform, approached by nine steps. The pharaoh's dress was a pleated white linen skirt and a golden breastplate and chain. On his head he wore the high red and white headpiece that he had adopted as his crown.

Pharaoh Ramses was an impressive looking man. He was clean shaven and strong. Moses knew from his childhood acquaintance with Ramses that he was energetic and smart.

Except for two slaves waving colorful ostrich fans, only one other person was on the platform with the pharaoh. At his right stood a twelve-year-old boy, whom Moses guessed was the pharaoh's son. He held his head high, knowing he was the crown prince. He was the son of Queen Asiyeh, Moses' Egyptian mother, whom Ramses had married so that his first-born son would have both parents descended from the pharaohs of Egypt.

Many people, officials of the court and friends of the

PHARAOH RAMSES WAS
AN IMPRESSIVE LOOKING MAN.

pharaoh, stood against the wall. Everything was clean, sweet-smelling, and showed how wealthy the pharaoh was. Even a pet lion yawned lazily in the corner.

Moses and Aaron bowed low before the pharaoh, stretching out their hands at knee level. Aaron had not wanted to do this, claiming it was not right, for they should bow only to God. Moses told him that bowing before a pharaoh showed respect for office rather than worshipping a god. Aaron had reluctantly agreed, but his bow was brief, almost sneering.

Before Moses could say, "Great Pharaoh, live forever," as he should when addressing the pharaoh, Ramses spoke.

"Well, Moses!" His high-pitched voice was calm, assured. "Tell me about that God of yours who talked to you at Mount Sinai. I believe His name is Yahweh."

The opening shot caught Moses off balance. It was cleverly done. Somehow the pharaoh knew everything about Moses. His spies must be everywhere. Moses knew he must be careful what he said to anybody from now on.

So. . .it was a battle of wits. Ramses thought he had won with this clever opening. But Moses had his own strategy. He lifted his head and spoke the words as strongly as he could: "Thus says Yahweh, 'Let My

"I BELIEVE HIS NAME IS YAHWEH."

people go!'"

He had come right to the point, and the issue was there before them. Around the audience hall, people gasped at his boldness. Everyone knew that Moses, a former Egyptian prince, was now a Josephite slave. They were fascinated by the conflict between the proud pharaoh on the throne and the bearded Sand Crosser nine steps below him.

Ramses smiled. He obviously enjoyed this. He had the advantage, and he knew it.

"Go where, Moses?" he asked placidly.

"We would like to go into the wilderness for three days to worship our God. Then we will return to our duties in Egypt."

This was the strategy Yahweh had told Moses. Not a bold demand for complete freedom, but just a three-day holiday. It might appeal to the pharaoh; a few days of rest might refresh his slaves and make them better workers.

Pharaoh Ramses was not impressed. "Who is Yahweh that I should listen to Him? I don't know any god named Yahweh." His voice was sarcastic. "Perhaps I shall ask Tait to slap Yahweh with her ostrich feather!"

All the Egyptians present laughed as they recognized

ALL THE EGYPTIANS LAUGHED.

the insult. Tait, a minor goddess of robes worn at a funeral, was sometimes pictured in shining clothing, including a magnificent ostrich feather. But Tait was such an unimportant goddess that people often made fun of her.

Moses clenched his fist and set his jaw, determined to hold his temper. But not Aaron. An insult to his God was taken personally, and before Moses could stop him, he strode forward to the foot of the steps leading up to the platform.

"Thus says Yahweh!" he thundered. "'If you don't let My people go, I will bring My wrath upon you and destroy you!'"

The people in the room gasped at these bold words. Nobody could talk to the pharaoh like that. The punishment would be instant death. The captain of the pharaoh's bodyguard drew his sword, but Ramses held up his hand. He leaned back on his throne, unruffled. In fact, he seemed pleased to have made one of the strange men before him so angry.

Very calmly, he stood up, holding high his golden scepter. Instantly the hall became quiet. The pharaoh of Egypt was about to make a decree.

"Let it be written, and let it be done!" The formal

MOSES CLENCHED HIS FIST.

words, the raising of the scepter, the authoritative tone of his voice: all present held their breaths. A scribe hastily assembled his materials and squatted to write.

"Behold, my slaves have become lazy. They play games with me. They demand a three-day holiday. Since, therefore, they do not have enough work to keep them busy, I hereby decree: They shall no longer have straw to make bricks, but the number of bricks they make must remain the same!"

Moses was stunned. It was a killing decree. Making bricks was a hard, time-consuming task of the slaves, as Moses knew from the past few weeks of labor with his family. Cruel taskmasters made them work hard, beating them if they did not make enough bricks. But now they would have to find their own straw. It would make their work even harder.

Aaron stepped forward to protest, but Moses stopped him with a hand on his shoulder. No one could object to a royal decree, once made. Spoken publicly, using official language, written down, it was now the law of the land.

With as much dignity as he could muster, Moses bowed before the pharaoh and turned to leave. Aaron didn't want to retreat, but after a moment's hesitation, he turned and meekly followed Moses. They marched with

MOSES STOPPED HIM.

heads high down the hall past the courtiers and out the door.

The pharaoh had won. His power was too much. It was no longer a contest of wits between Moses and Ramses. It was a question of power. And Ramses sat on the throne.

Where was God? Moses sighed, feeling deflated, defeated. He had lost. No, he had not lost. God had lost.

What had happened to the Presence he had felt so clearly on the mountain? Where was Yahweh now, when it counted?

As the days went by, Moses' doubts grew stronger. Without straw, the people could not make enough bricks to meet their quotas. The slave drivers whipped the Israelite foremen in charge of the work crews. "Lazy dogs!" they shouted. "You haven't met your quotas again today."

At last the Israelite foremen went to Pharaoh to plead with him. But Pharaoh would not listen. Frustrated and discouraged, the foremen then complained to Moses.

"This is all your fault," one of them said.

"That's right," said another. "Because of you, Pharaoh won't even listen to us. When we talked to him,

MOSES' DOUBTS GREW STRONGER.

he acted as though he smelled something rotten and then he said 'Get back to work!' and turned away."

Another muttered, "I hope you're happy. Now you've given Pharaoh an excuse to kill us."

Moses tried to explain what Yahweh had told him, but his words stumbled over each other. The foremen shook their heads in disgust. "You're crazy. We don't have time to listen to you. We have to find straw for tomorrow's work."

That night Moses sat alone outside, staring up at the starry sky. "I'm not helping my people," he whispered. "I'   only making things worse." He pounded his staff   ...e ground in frustration. "Are You real, Yahweh? Or are those foremen right? Am I crazy?"

Suddenly the night was filled with that same overwhelming Presence he had experienced on the mountain. *I AM.* The Voice was calm. *I am the One who spoke to Abraham, Isaac, and Jacob. I made a promise to them—and I will keep My promise. Tell the Israelites that they are special to Me. I will free them from their slavery and I will give them their own land. Remember, Moses—I AM. Go tell Pharaoh to let My people go.*

"Why should Pharaoh listen to me when my own people think I'm crazy?" Moses remembered the way he

"I'M NOT HELPING MY PEOPLE."

had stumbled and stuttered when he had tried to explain Yahweh's message to the Israelite foremen. His face flushed. "I'm not good at speaking, God. There's no use in me trying to persuade Pharaoh. I'll just mumble and stammer, and he won't listen to me."

Go, the Voice insisted calmly. *Tell Pharaoh to let My people go. Take Aaron with you if you're too scared to trust Me. Let him use your staff. But go.*

GO, THE VOICE INSISTED CALMLY.

BUT RAMSES WAS NOT IMPRESSED.

10

The next day, Aaron and Moses went to talk to Pharaoh. Outside the palace door, Moses handed Aaron his staff.

"What's this for?" Aaron asked.

Moses shrugged. "I'm not sure. Just be ready to do whatever I tell you."

Inside the court, Aaron stood proudly before Pharaoh Ramses. "The God of Israel says to you, 'Let My people go!'" His voice thundered through the great hall.

But Ramses was not impressed. He picked idly at his thumbnail. "Why should I?"

"Because our God is powerful," answered Aaron, "and with His power He will destroy you if you do not do as He says."

Ramses yawned. "Prove it. Prove that your God is powerful and that He has sent me this message."

All at once, Moses knew what to do. "Throw the staff onto the floor," he whispered into Aaron's ear.

Aaron glanced at him as though he were crazy, but then he lifted the staff over his head and flung it down.

It clattered across the shiny tile, and then, just as it had on the mountain, it changed. A long, dark snake slithered toward Pharaoh's throne.

Ramses drew his feet up under him. His eyes were wide and dark for an instant, but then he waved his hand to one of his servants. "Call my magicians," he said.

In a few minutes, the space beside the throne was crowded with Pharaoh's wise men and magicians. In front of the throne, the snake coiled and uncoiled restlessly while the magicians whispered together. Moses watched the snake, wondering what would happen next.

Suddenly he realized that the floor was covered with writhing, twining shapes. Snakes slithered and twisted around the throne. Pharaoh clapped his hands and laughed. "Look, Israelites. My wise men can do the same trick."

And then he fell silent. The entire room was quiet, watching as one by one the first snake swallowed up all the others. After only a few minutes, once again only one snake coiled and uncoiled on the shiny floor. Pharaoh shifted uneasily on his throne.

"Pick it up," Moses whispered in Aaron's ear. "Tell Pharaoh that if he does not obey God, you will use the staff to bring down plagues on Egypt."

132

**SNAKES SLITHERED AND TWISTED
AROUND THE THRONE.**

Aaron hesitated only a moment, and then with a flourish he picked up the snake. Instantly, it became a staff once more. The wise men and magicians murmured to each other. Aaron's voice rose loud and clear above their whispers. "Let My people go so they can worship Me in the wilderness, thus says Yahweh, God of Israel." He raised the staff high above his head, and then he warned Pharaoh of the coming plagues.

When the first disaster happened, the Israelites in Goshen saw the water of the Great River and all its small branches in the delta turn red.

"What is it?" they asked.

"A plague," they decided. "The first of many. Yahweh is showing the pharaoh His power."

It was hard to return to work. Moses' blood churned and his heart pounded with excitement. God was at work.

But he had to make bricks.

He joined Aaron at the brick works and patiently poured mud into straw-filled molds, placed them in the sun to bake, then removed and stacked them. Hour after hour. Day after day. Week after week.

Nevertheless, things were happening. God's hand rested heavily on the land of Egypt. There was no flood

HE WARNED PHARAOH OF THE COMING PLAGUES.

that year, but the water was polluted by the blood red tide. No one could drink the waters of the Great River.

The Israelites experienced no inconvenience. They had long been accustomed to digging wells, and wherever they went there were deep-dug sources of pure water. The land of Goshen had hundreds of them. The people of Egypt who had laughed at them for digging wells were not laughing now. They were digging wells, too.

Then came the frogs. They came out of the Great River and spread across the Black Lands, carrying filth and disease with them. They died, and the land stank with their rotting bodies. Egyptians, being clean people, couldn't stand it.

The mosquitoes and sand gnats came next. They were everywhere. People slapped and scratched. Painful sores appeared on their bodies, and no amount of washing would clear them up. They prayed. They sacrificed. They begged their gods for relief. But the troubles continued.

Even in Goshen the mosquitoes were bad. Moses then showed the Israelites a remedy that the Sand Crossers used. He made a paste of roots and water. The Egyptians would never put this on their body because it would mean not having their daily bath, and the paste

THEN CAME THE FROGS.

smelled almost as bad as the dead frogs. Moses could understand the feeling, having been raised in Egypt. But in the desert he had learned that daily bathing was a waste of water, and the foul smell of the paste was better than the insect bites and the resulting skin diseases.

The Israelites accepted the paste with good cheer, for it was a time of good cheer, even in their daily toil. They worked hard from dawn until dusk, doing backbreaking, monotonous chores, but they did so with songs and laughter. They had hope. They looked around at the awful things happening to the Egyptian people and smiled knowingly. God was at work. They would soon be free.

When the cattle began to die in the fields everywhere in Egypt except among the Israelite herds in Goshen, people began to whisper that word: Yahweh. All up and down the Great River, people talked about this mysterious new God.

Other terrible things happened in Egypt. A devastating hailstorm destroyed the barley crop, which the people depended on for much of their diet. Then a swarm of locusts swept in from the eastern desert, eating the wheat crop, and Egypt faced famine and starvation. But not in Goshen. The storm from the south did not reach Goshen,

A SWARM OF LOCUSTS SWEPT IN.

and a north wind kept the locusts away from the gardens of the Israelites.

Finally came the sandstorm, bringing a darkness even in the daytime. The sand thickened the air, biting the skin. Many livestock died; but in Goshen, where they had been warned, the animals stayed safely in their barns.

Moses had become acquainted with the overseer of the work crew at the construction site at Raamses. He was an educated, intelligent man from a good family. Since the plagues began, he, like everybody else in Egypt, began to treat the slaves kindly, and he spoke to Moses with respect.

He often discussed with Moses the affairs of Egypt. One day he mentioned that the chief magician in Ramses' court had quit. Just walked out.

"The wise man," the overseer said scornfully, "admitted that these plagues are not tricks a clever magician could explain. He wants nothing more to do with this contest." He stroked his smooth chin. "Everybody in Egypt is suffering."

Moses nodded. "They suffer because of Ramses. When will he admit that Yahweh is more powerful than even a pharaoh?"

"All Egypt speaks of you, Moses," the overseer said.

"EVERYBODY IN EGYPT IS SUFFERING."

"What have you heard?"

"They say you and your God are sending the plagues upon Egypt. First you withheld the annual flood. Then you turned the water into blood, which polluted the waters. You called the frogs up from the Great River to march across the land, to die and rot and stink and make our lives miserable."

Moses said nothing, waiting for him to continue.

"Then you picked up some dust and threw it into the air, and it turned into swarms of gnats and mosquitoes that spread over the land. You struck down much of our livestock with disease, and you caused our skin to break out with sores and rashes. You waved your staff, causing a hailstorm, locust swarm, and a sandstorm. Egypt is suffering, Moses, and the people are saying it is you and your God who are doing it."

Moses nodded. He already knew what the people were saying about him. He was primarily interested in this educated, thoughtful man's reaction to these events.

"Is it true, Moses?" he asked.

"Only partly true, my friend. Actually, it's God alone who does these things. I'm only a bystander, a representative of Yahweh who speaks before the pharaoh."

"The pharaoh." He frowned. "And how does he feel

"IS IT TRUE, MOSES?"

about this? Do you think he'll give you your freedom?"

Moses nodded. "He'll give in. Soon now. There's one more plague to come. . .the worst one."

His eyebrows raised slightly. Was there a hint of fear in his eyes? He looked around. Moses followed his gaze. Not far off stood a young man who was one of the taskmasters. He was a handsome youth, also educated, with a fine future. Moses knew who he was: the overseer's first-born son.

"Moses, let's speak frankly for a moment." The overseer spoke without taking his eyes off his son. "We're both intelligent people. We know what is really happening."

Moses said nothing. He waited respectfully.

"The flood failed this year. Nothing miraculous about that; it happens seldom, but it has happened before. And the water did not really turn to blood; the red tide from the south comes at the end of every summer. The difference is that the flood water was not there to dilute it and wash it away."

Moses again said nothing, waiting to hear the rest.

"The frogs came out of the river seeking fresh water, carrying with them diseases and impurities from the polluted water. They spread across the land, causing

MOSES KNEW WHO HE WAS.

the cattle to sicken and die in the fields. Because there was no flood, the gnats and mosquitoes are exceptionally bad this year, which caused the sores and rashes on the people. All natural."

He paused, still looking at his son. "Moses, we know most Egyptians are superstitious people. They will believe anything. But you and I are rational, educated, and clear thinking. We know what is really happening."

A moment of doubt flickered across Moses' mind. Denying miracles, ridiculing the superstitious people. Once he had thought just as this man did. What was the overseer really saying? Something unspoken, behind his logical words?

Moses said, "You and I are basically different people. I believe in Yahweh, that He is doing these things. It is God who is the basic cause of Egypt's problems."

Again Moses caught the slight flicker of the overseer's eyebrow and a tightening of his jaw muscles. Why? Did he believe that the former Egyptian prince, now the leader of the Josephites, had turned into a religious fanatic? Or. . .was he afraid?

"Of course, you're right, Moses. It all depends on your point of view, your starting place. And when famine comes, you will say Yahweh has cursed Egypt."

"YOU'RE RIGHT, MOSES."

The overseer turned to face Moses. "But Moses . . ." He paused. "Moses, if what you say is true, then we are at the mercy of the whims of this God of yours. What's to stop Him from. . .from. . .doing anything?"

Suddenly he was unmasked. His aristocratic pose, his logical reasoning, his insistence upon believing in an ordered way of life—it was all a front. He was trying desperately to convince himself, not Moses, that there was no God in the picture. And he was failing.

He turned abruptly and stared over at his son. Moses' arm rested gently on his shoulders.

"My friend, what's really troubling you?"

He turned to face Moses, anguish in his eyes. "Moses. . .please?" He drew a deep breath. "Spare my first-born son!"

The words hung in the late afternoon stillness. The impact of his statement struck Moses like a blow of a club, and he recoiled under its force. His first-born son! And not only his, but all the first-born sons of Egypt! In that brief word, God showed Moses the future.

He now knew what the final plague would be. Maybe this was God's way of revealing the truth to him.

"My friend, I . . ." He paused. What could he say? "I'm sorry. I have no control over Yahweh. In fact, it's

"SPARE MY FIRST-BORN SON!"

He who controls me. There's nothing I can do."

The overseer nodded, saying nothing. He only stared at his son, his face a mask. Then he smiled.

"This is absurd, Moses. I'm being superstitious, like those. . .people. It's foolish of me."

"Friend. . .may Yahweh give you peace."

He smiled. "Thank you, Moses." Then he turned and walked away.

"FRIEND.. MAY YAHWEH GIVE YOU PEACE."

"WE MUST MAKE PREPARATIONS."

11

It was time to go. After this last plague, the pharaoh would give his Josephite slaves the freedom they demanded. And—Moses knew—it would begin tonight.

He spread the word among the Israelites that the time had come, and he wanted to meet with the elders immediately. A fever of excitement and enthusiasm gripped everyone. The elders reflected it as they came together for the meeting.

"Is it true, Moses?" they asked. At his assurance, they grinned and nodded. They were ready.

Aaron spoke. "The people are already packing. They'll be ready to go tomorrow. They've been ready for months."

Moses already knew this. But he had to warn them. "It's also a time of danger for us. We must make preparations."

They were full of questions. What will cause the pharaoh to let us go? Is it the last plague? Will it happen tonight? What did he mean by danger for us?

Moses knew he must explain what was ahead. And

it had to be done right, exactly right, not only for their protection, but that it might be remembered. He must give them something to tell their children and grandchildren. Some kind of sign of God's power, never to be forgotten.

The last elders shuffled in, hurrying on rheumatic legs. Their eager faces turned to him expectantly.

"People of Israel," he began. "We leave tomorrow."

There were nods but no further reactions. They already knew that. What else?

"Tonight is the night of the final plague. It will be the worst of all."

A deep silence now settled on the group. Nobody moved. Every face reflected eagerness. Moses had no time for eloquence. That was Aaron's specialty; now he had to speak clearly, so they would be sure to understand.

"Tonight, God will pass over Egypt with a heavy hand, bringing death to all the first-born sons!"

Murmurs of excitement rippled through the crowd, but soon turned to fear as they realized what this meant.

"Will we escape?" asked one, voicing the concern of all.

Moses nodded. "Listen carefully to my instructions

"TONIGHT IS THE NIGHT OF THE FINAL PLAGUE."

and follow them exactly. Let each family take a lamb and kill it in front of their house. The lamb must be perfect. Let it be offered as a sacrifice to Yahweh."

The people listened carefully, a little frightened.

"Each head of the household shall take a branch of hyssop and sprinkle the blood of the sacrificial lamb on the door posts of his house. Let each family go inside. Bar the door. Shutter the windows. Then when God's hand cuts down the children of Egypt tonight, He will see the houses of the faithful and pass over, leaving them unharmed."

The elders nodded silently, recognizing the importance of what he said. *This night will be remembered always,* thought Moses.

"Tonight, we must eat unleavened bread. Bake your bread today without yeast, because we can't wait for the yeast to rise. Roast the sacrificial lamb and eat it for your supper. Eat it all, with nothing left over. We must leave at sunrise tomorrow."

The people listened in awe. They would remember tonight.

"Tomorrow we will gather on the plain of the construction site of Raamses. There we will camp for the first night and organize for the march."

THE PEOPLE LISTENED IN AWE.

The meeting was over, but Aaron wasn't ready to leave yet. He had been standing quietly while Moses spoke. But now he had something to say. Moses hoped it wouldn't be long. They had a lot of work to do.

"Blessed be Yahweh, the God of Israel, for He visits and redeems His people. O give thanks to Yahweh, for He is good; His steadfast love endures forever. Let the redeemed of Yahweh say so, and praise His name forever and ever!"

The benediction over, the people turned to hurry home. Moses again marveled at Aaron's ability to say the right thing at the right time. The closing words were exactly what was needed. They, too, would be remembered forever.

THE CLOSING WORDS WERE EXACTLY
WHAT WAS NEEDED.

HE SAW A STRANGE COLUMN OF SMOKE.

12

The next day, the people gathered at the construction site of the city of Raamses, all packed and eager to go. Nothing had happened to them during the night. But today no taskmasters were at the job site. Nobody stopped them. In fact, Moses saw no Egyptians at all, but he heard the sounds of wailing and sobbing. He knew why. The Egyptians were in mourning today—for their first-born sons.

The next day, the Israelites traveled across Egypt toward the desert. There were so many of them! Moses wondered how they would ever make it through the wilderness. He felt weighed down by his responsibility for all these people.

And then he lifted his head and saw a strange column of smoke hovering in the air before him. Moses gripped Aaron's arm. "What is that?"

Aaron shrugged. "It has been before us all day." When night fell, the column of smoke began to shine, a strange red glow that led them on and on into the wilderness. They had left Egypt far behind.

After several days, they encamped at the Reed Sea. Moses knew that the column of smoke and fire was leading them south, to the narrow strip of land between the Lake of the Crocodiles and the Lesser Bitter Lake, where they would leave the fertile country of the Great River. Then. . .the desert.

As the day lazily moved toward evening, a peaceful camp scene emerged. Smoke from cooking fires filtered slowly up to the sky. Livestock contentedly grazed on the nearby grasslands or wandered down to the shore of the Reed Sea to drink. Men and women busily moved around doing the camping chores. There was a babble of conversation and even some laughter. The camp settled down early; and as the sun began to set behind the western dunes, streaking the sky with pink and red, a weary stillness pressed down upon them. They had become accustomed to the strange fiery smoke that hovered over them; no one paid any attention to it tonight.

Suddenly a woman screamed and pointed. Something was happening behind them, to the north. People turned to look. Men shouted, women shrieked, children wailed, and the livestock bleated.

Moses swung around and faced the north. There at the top of the dune was a sight that sent a shiver up his

SUDDENLY A WOMAN SCREAMED
AND POINTED.

spine. A line of chariots had drawn up on the crest of the hill, silhouetted against the red sky. Egyptian chariots, silent and unmoving, staring down at the encamped Israelites.

There must be at least six hundred of them. Moses gaped at them. The horses were snorting and pawing the sand. The big chariots had deadly scythes attached to the axles. Three men were in each chariot: a driver, a shield bearer, and a warrior. They were only half a mile away.

The people panicked. They ran everywhere, screaming. Women clutched their children; men grabbed makeshift weapons, gripping them awkwardly. Moses tried to calm them, but they were so frightened, they wouldn't listen.

The Egyptians did not attack, knowing the Israelites had no place to go. Daylight tomorrow would be plenty of time for the killing.

Darkness came. Families huddled together, trembling and crying. Moses stood under a palm tree, wondering what to do. No breath of air stirred the waters of the lake at this moment. The night was as calm and still as could be. All at once Moses knew what God wanted him to tell the people. He cleared his throat to speak, but the words wouldn't come; they made no sense. *Speak,*

A LINE OF CHARIOTS HAD DRAWN UP.

insisted the Presence that was always with him. Moses cleared his throat again.

"Be ready to leave in the middle watch," he told the people. "We'll cross the lake here and get away from them." He stretched his staff across the quiet water; then he turned away and walked into the darkness.

He found a palm tree where he could sit and be alone. Under it, in its dark shadow, he could hide. And maybe rest. Would they be able to cross? Yahweh, are You really there? You're not just my imagination?

Moses leaned back against the palm tree and sighed. He was so tired! He'd sit here for just a short time. His eyelids drooped, and he closed them for a moment. Just a moment. He mustn't stay here long. But he needed this brief time of relaxation.

Sleep finally found him, deep refreshing slumber. He slept on into the night, not yet aware of the wind whipping his hair and beard and ruffling his robe, a brisk wind out of the east.

"Moses! Moses!"

A voice was calling him from far away. It was urgent, insistent. He wanted to ignore it, but he couldn't.

"Moses! Look!"

He opened his eyes and looked around. A babble of

YAHWEH, ARE YOU REALLY THERE?

voices and excitement surrounded him. He looked where people were pointing, out into the moonlight. . .the Sea of Reeds. There was the lake bed, with no water in it.

He came suddenly awake. The lake bed! It was dry!

The strong east wind blew in his face as he pulled himself groggily to his feet, holding on to the palm tree. On stiff legs he hobbled out of the shadow toward the Sea of Reeds. Slogging about ten paces into the muddy lake bottom, he felt the wet sand suck up around his sandals. It was soft, slimy, and shifting; but he could walk on it. Enough rocks and stones at the bottom gave support.

"Pass the word. We leave as soon as we can. Every family should cross the lake bed directly from your campsite."

The crowd burst into a furor of activity. They ran, shouting the news as they went. The feverish energy continued around the camp; even in the darkness, Moses was aware of the bustle of activity. Men shouted, women called their children, babies cried, young voices complained, sheep bleated. The multitude began to move.

Moses watched, fascinated, as a man and a boy drove the first herd of sheep into the lake bed. The sheep were reluctant, their feet sinking into the mud. The man and boy ran behind on their flanks, shouting, waving

THE LAKE BED! IT WAS DRY!

their arms. A girl joined them, clapping her hands and adding her shrill voice. The sheep pushed on into the sea of mud.

A wagon pulled by oxen bogged down about twenty feet from the shore. A man pushed the ox cart and a woman pulled on one beast's harness. The animal bawled in protest. But it moved; the wheels turned, and they went on.

It was all happening at once. As far as Moses could see in the darkness, people and animals were moving out. The confused noise was loud, but it was orderly. The sea of people and wagons and livestock were on their way.

Finally, it was time for him to go.

Out on the lake bed, the people were struggling. They were halfway across, but the going was tough. There were no more shouts now; the men were gasping with fatigue as they battled the reluctant animals and the sucking mud. Many of them—men, women, and children—carried lambs in their arms. It was a slow trek, but they were moving.

Moses marched out into the lake bed. The mud oozed up around his sandals, gripping his feet. He was alone, with no animals to herd before him, no family to keep track of, no wagon to push through the mud, no lamb to

THE PEOPLE WERE STRUGGLING.

carry. He had only himself, yet he found the going very difficult. What must it have been like for the others? The sandy bottom had been churned up by hundreds of feet and hooves. He had trouble pulling his sandals free from the mud. Each step was a battle in itself, and his muscles ached.

Halfway across, he heard a soft bleat. Looking around, he saw a lamb half-buried in the mire. Wide eyes stared at Moses. He stumbled back a few steps to the animal and worked it free from its muddy prison. Straining, he picked it up and carried it in his arms, the sand and slime from the lake bottom soiling his clothes. Once he stumbled and fell, landing heavily on the squalling lamb. He pushed to his feet, picked up his burden, and went on.

A hundred yards from the opposite shore—it seemed as though he had been traveling like this forever. His breath came in gasps and his muscles ached. One more step. Another. Another. He could not think beyond the next step.

The night was graying into dawn. Moses heard a shout ahead of him and looked up. The people had all reached the opposite bank and were staring back, pointing, yelling, waving. At him? No—something behind him.

HE WORKED IT FREE FROM ITS MUDDY PRISON.

He turned around. It was light enough to see across the lake now, through the mist rising from the lake bed. At the far shore, where he had entered, were the Egyptian chariots. As he watched, he could hear a shouted order. The horses plunged in, their chariots bouncing behind. The three occupants in each chariot where ghostly in the misty dawn.

They're coming. Moses gripped the lamb tighter, causing it to bleat in protest. If the Israelites could cross, so could the Egyptians. It would be harder for them, with their horses and chariots. But they could do it. And his people couldn't go anywhere. They were doomed.

But this was no time to panic. He still had to cross the remaining eighty yards of lake bed. The brief stop to look back had mired his feet deeply in the mud. He pulled out his right foot. The thought of the Egyptians behind him drove him on. One step, pull out the foot, another step. He lost his sandals, but they were useless to him now. Stones cut his feet, and he left bloody footsteps. The lamb in his arms was a dead weight. Still fifty yards to go.

He looked ahead. The mass of people lining the shore were pointing, shouting, moaning, sobbing, tearing their clothes. What's happening? He jerked a hurried

AT THE FAR SHORE WERE
THE EGYPTIAN CHARIOTS.

glance over his shoulder. The Egyptians were in the middle now, struggling. All three men from each chariot had descended, one pulling at the horse's head, the other two pushing at the chariot's wheels. The horses were floundering, the chariots sinking deeper; but they were moving. Pushing ahead. Slowly getting closer.

Yet something was different. It was almost full light, and the sun was just beginning to push its fiery ball over the eastern horizon. But there something else that was different, some change. . .the wind! It was no longer from the east! It was from the west!

The water! Would the breeze turn the water back? He looked toward the west, where the water had been backed up. Yes! It was coming, a vast tidal wave plunging toward him. He looked ahead: twenty yards to go. He couldn't make it.

He braced himself as the wave hit him. The force of it knocked him to his knees, and he had to drop one arm from the lamb to catch himself on the muddy bottom. His knees were cut by stones, but he felt no pain as the water flooded over him.

He struggled to his feet, gasping for breath. The water came to his waist, but it was quickly going down. The main force of the wave had passed, and there was

HE BRACED HIMSELF AS THE WAVE HIT HIM.

shallow bottom now. He still held the lamb, which continued to bleat.

Step forward. Another. He was wading, but it was easier, and the water was below his knees. A man from the shore ran into the water and took the lamb from him. Then two others were there, one on each side, holding his arms, helping him the last few steps. He was at the shore. He collapsed on the ground, exhausted, his chest heaving.

"Moses! Look!" People were pointing and shouting and laughing and clapping. He turned around. The mist had lifted, and all he could see was water where the dry lake bed had been.

The chariots! Where were they? There, in the middle. A horse, plunging and screaming; a man, his plumed helmet gone, crying to his gods for help; an overturned chariot, its wheel above the water turning weirdly. A few scenes like that, but no chariot squadron. They were gone.

A few soldiers made it back to the far shore, dripping and frightened and exhausted. *Good,* thought Moses. *They'll tell Ramses about the power of Yahweh.* Surely this was the end of it. Nobody would dare bother them now.

THE CHARIOTS! WHERE WERE THEY?

He became aware of a strange silence. The Israelites had ceased their shouting and were frozen in awe as the realization of what had happened burst upon them.

In the stillness, a sweet soprano voice—Miriam's—rose in the clear morning air: "O sing to Yahweh, our redeemer, for He has triumphed gloriously! The horse and its rider He has flung into the sea!"

THE ISRAELITES WERE FROZEN IN AWE.

THE PEOPLE WERE NOT USED TO DESERT TRAVEL.

13

The desert was hard, as Moses knew it would be. He was the only one in that vast company of people who knew its secrets. Once again he was reminded of God's wisdom, leading him here for many years to learn the mysteries of the desert from his father-in-law, Jethro.

The people were not used to desert travel. They had been slaves, living in mud-brick houses, tending their sheep or their gardens, working at building the city of Raamses. But that was not very good preparation for wilderness travel. Many of them, especially the Egyptians who had come along with them, began to drop out and return to Egypt. A few of the Israelites preferred to return to being slaves in Egypt rather than live the harsh life of the desert.

For the desert was harsh. But thanks to Moses, they learned how to live there.

With all of these secrets of the desert, Moses taught his people the same lesson Jethro had taught him: all the gifts came from Yahweh, who protected them. He taught them to walk with their heads up, seeing God, not merely down, seeing the desert. And God provided for His people in mysterious ways.

Probably the most fascinating mystery happened one night as they camped at an oasis with a lot of tamarisk trees. The people were hungry and complained to Moses.

"Did you bring us out here to starve to death, Moses?" they asked. "We were better off as slaves in Egypt."

Moses sighed. They forgot so quickly how God took care of them. Well, they would just have to learn again.

"Tomorrow morning," he told them, "you will again see the power of God. He will give you bread to eat."

Nobody believed him, but they were too much in awe of him to say anything. They were surprised the next morning when they awoke to find white flaky stuff on the ground! When they tasted it, they were delighted at its sweetness.

"What is it?" they asked.

The word in their language for "what is it" was man-hu. After Moses explained that it was a gift from God, they called it "manna" for short.

The desert was cruel, but their greatest test still lay ahead. Every once in a while, Moses glimpsed in the distance some men. He knew who they were. Amalekites!

Sooner or later, they would have to fight them. But

IT WAS A GIFT FROM GOD.

the Israelites were not fighters. They had never learned how to use a spear. In fact, they had no weapons. Once again, Moses thanked God for preparing him for leadership, for he knew how to fight and could teach them.

Some of the Israelites were carpenters and metalsmiths, and Moses put them to work making spears. Then began the training. They were encamped at a large oasis called Rephidim, and there Moses taught them the art of spear fighting. They were clumsy at first, but with patience they learned.

Then Moses learned from the scouts he had sent out that the Amalekites were coming. There were a lot of them. Moses suspected that the five brothers who had bothered the daughters of Jethro were their leaders, and they had gone to the land of the Amalekites and recruited a vast army. They outnumbered the Israelites. It would be a difficult battle.

So Moses, who had been trained in military tactics when he was a young Egyptian prince, chose the battlefield. It was a long narrow valley, with steep wooded hills on both sides. There he would set a trap for the enemy.

He stationed his men on both sides of the valley, hidden in the trees. He gave them a set of signals, a series of trumpet blasts.

MOSES PUT THEM TO WORK MAKING SPEARS.

Then they settled down to wait. This was the hardest part. The men were eager to fight, but without the surprise of an ambush, they would be at a disadvantage because the enemy outnumbered them.

All through the night they waited. In the morning, they heard the Amalekites coming. They were trotting along, singing a war chant. They looked fierce.

Moses waited until just the right moment. When the Amalekite army was all in the narrow valley, he nodded to Aaron, who raised his trumpet to his lips. The long, wailing note blared out over the valley.

Instantly, his men attacked. They poured down the hillside and hurled themselves at the enemy. The Amalekites were surprised, and many were killed in the first onrush. But they fought back, and they fought fiercely.

He saw an Israelite battling against two Amalekites. Fighting the way Moses had taught him, he danced around nimbly, thrusting with his spear. He killed one Amalekite, but the other was able to get behind him and hit him hard on the head with his club. The brave Israelite warrior went down, badly wounded.

This was only one small scene Moses witnessed. There were many others. The battle was going badly for

THEY POURED DOWN THE HILLSIDE.

the Israelites, and the enemy was winning because of their numbers.

Then came a lull in the battle, as everyone paused for a moment to catch their breath. Moses stood on a rock and raised his arms, his staff in hand.

"Yahweh!" he shouted as loud as he could.

The men renewed the battle, and it seemed that the name of God, which Moses had shouted, gave them strength. They fought harder and seemed to be winning. And yet there were so many Amalekites, it seemed unlikely the Israelites could win. But then they would look up and see Moses standing there on the rock above them, shouting encouragement, his staff lifted high.

Moses grew tired, though, and his arms sagged. When the Israelites looked up, they no longer could see his staff dark against the sky. Tiredness washed over the Israelite army and they began to lose ground.

Then Aaron and another man climbed up beside Moses and held up Moses' arms. They, too, cheered the warriors and offered prayers to God.

Slowly the tide of battle turned, and the Israelites seemed to be winning. *Yes,* thought Moses, *they were winning!* But their victory came with a terrible price.

All up and down the battlefield lay the dead and

AARON AND ANOTHER MAN
HELD UP MOSES' ARMS.

wounded. When the battle was over and the last Amalekite was killed, Moses cried out in despair as he saw the large number of young men who were either dead or badly hurt.

"Hurry, Aaron!" he said. "Run back to the camp and tell the women to bring stretchers. We must save as many of them as we can!"

Moses came down into the valley of death. So many dead! Not just Israelites but also Amalekites. There were the five brothers, sprawled in death among their comrades. And there were the Israelites. So young. So much of their lives ahead of them. Now gone. Dead. Gone forever.

"War!" muttered Moses as he knelt to help a wounded Israelite warrior. "Nobody wins in war. We might win one battle, but in war, everybody loses!"

He decided that from that day on, he would do everything he could to avoid fighting. It just wasn't worth it!

"IN WAR, EVERYBODY LOSES!"

MOSES EMBRACED HIS WIFE.

14

Moses kept the Israelites at Rephidim for several months because that was the only oasis in the area that was big enough for so large a group of people. They needed the time to recover from the battle.

Moses missed his family. He wished Zipporah were with him to share all the adventures and hardships and excitement of the long trek through the wilderness. He wondered how Gershom was, and it startled him to realize that he might even have another child now; he didn't even know if it was a boy or a girl.

One day, while Moses sat in the judgment seat setling disputes that the people brought to him, he had a visitor. Jethro! And Jethro had brought Zipporah with him!

Moses ran to his wife and embraced her. He had missed her so much! At last they were reunited. Gershom had grown and become strong and Zipporah and Gershom proudly showed him the new baby—a boy! Now Moses had two sons. He decided to name the second son Eliezer, meaning "God has helped me," remembering how God had helped him not only in the past year, but all of his life.

Moses longed to see the mountain where he had first met God. It was not very far away from Rephidim, but he had been so busy he hadn't had time to go there. Now that Jethro was there to help organize the people and settle some of the disputes, perhaps he could go. Later, he would bring the people to the mountain to let them see for themselves the awesome mountain and possibly experience something of what Moses had felt there.

So Moses left, promising to be back in a few days. He made the journey alone, and soon came to the mountain the Sand Crossers called Horeb and the Egyptians called Sinai.

As he climbed the mountain, he thought about his people. They were now a large nation, and they needed laws. Every nation needed laws, and soon the Israelites would have a land of their own. Laws would help them govern themselves.

And so he began to think about laws for his people. All kinds of laws: how to worship God properly, how to live with other people. Laws about punishments, about sickness, about priests, about worship. So many things. But what they needed most of all was a simple set of

HE CLIMBED THE MOUNTAIN.

rules that would be the basis for all the other laws. God, give us the laws we need.

When he reached the top of the mountain, he was once again impressed with the feeling he had. The silence—the overwhelming silence—and the feeling that he was not alone. This time, however, he understood the feeling. God was there. And God would give him the laws he needed.

And the night came upon him, suddenly and without warning. And with the night came a storm. He had never before been on the mountain in a storm. Once a cloud cover had come upon him, but never a storm. He had no idea it would be so fierce.

Moses huddled in a cleft of a rock while the wind blew and the rain pelted down. Thunder rumbled, and distant lightning flashes crackled and sparked. And that eerie sensation that he was not alone was stronger than ever. Why was it he felt so weird? Was it the storm?

Suddenly the sky before him split open in a blinding flash of lightning. In the gigantic gash that ripped across the black night, he caught a glimpse of another universe, a completely unknown world, through the jagged slit in the wall of darkness. Then the black sides of night clashed back over it, erupting in a tremendous blast of

MOSES HUDDLED IN A CLEFT OF A ROCK

deafening thunder. He cringed before it.

Again the lightning splashed furiously across the sky, its brightness shattering the dark curtain of night. The thunder clap followed so closely that it seemed a continuation of the first one. Again a vivid flash, sharp and dazzling, and at the same time a crack of thunder.

He didn't know how long it continued. He felt himself fading away, the angry tempest receding from his view. He drifted for a while, then consciousness returned.

And silence. Gone was the thundering roar of the tempest, the vivid brilliance of the lightning flashes. Something was different, so different he couldn't identify it at first. Then suddenly he knew. He looked around in awe.

He wasn't alone. The Presence was there. Never before had he experienced Yahweh so intensely. He felt a complete and total peace, deep and satisfying. And in the midst of this peace, he heard Yahweh's Voice.

Tell the Israelites: See how I have borne you up on eagles' wings and brought you here to Myself. Now listed—if you will keep My covenant, you shall be My special people, a holy nation.

"But what is Your covenant, Lord?" Moses asked.

I will tell you, the Voice said, *in three days. Tell the*

"BUT WHAT IS YOUR COVENANT, LORD?"

people to get ready. They should wash their clothes—and they should examine their hearts. On the third day have the people wait at the foot of the mountain while you climb to the top. They will see a great cloud and hear My Voice while I give to you the covenant of My law.

So Moses went back down the mountain and told the people what Yahweh had said, and everyone did just as Moses told them. On the third day, men and women and children all waited at the foot of the mountain, dressed in clean clothes with shiny faces, while Moses again climbed the mountain.

When he came back, he brought with him the Ten Commandments that God had given him, written on tablets of stone.

The people looked at him with awe and amazement, and even Zipporah, Moses' wife, stared at him with round eyes.

"Did you hear God's Voice speaking?" Moses asked her.

Zipporah shook her head. "The mountain smoked and trembled. We heard a horrible loud noise, like thunder and trumpets mixed together." Her eyes were troubled. "I was frightened, Moses. This God you talk with—" She shook

HE BROUGHT WITH HIM
THE TEN COMMANDMENTS.

her head again. "I think I might die if I spoke with Him as you do."

Moses put his hand on his wife's shoulder. "Yahweh loves us, Zipporah. So long as we obey His laws, we do not need to fear Him. He has promised to watch over us and our children—and our children's children forever."

Jethro had been listening and now he nodded his head. He raised his brows as he met Moses' eyes. "So, Moses, at last you have set aside your dependence on logic and science."

Moses smiled at his father-in-law. "I know now that God gave humanity both science and logic—but Yahweh is bigger than either. We cannot put Him into a box where we can explain away His mighty works. He is just too big." He touched Zipporah's face. "But He loves us. This immense God loves us."

"YAHWEH LOVES US, ZIPPORAH."

SURELY GOD WAS IN THIS PLACE!

15

With the new laws, Israel became a nation. Now they were ready to go to the Promised Land. Moses, with Jethro's help, organized a system of judges, a tent for worship called the Tabernacle, a priesthood, a plan for the Sabbath Day, and everything else a nation needed to be successful.

And they began their trek through the wilderness to the Promised Land. Moses guessed the trip would take less than a year. They passed by the mountain that had meant so much to Moses, and as they did so, a thunderstorm struck the peak. The people were awed by what they saw. Surely God was in this place! Moses had to assure them that God was not only there but with them wherever they went. The column of smoke and fire continued to lead them, convincing the people that Moses spoke the truth.

After a long and hard struggle with the wilderness, they came to a large oasis called Kadesh-Barnea, not very far from their Promised Land. Moses decided to send out scouts to see the land that lay ahead of them.

He chose twelve young men who seemed eager for the adventure. He told them to go all through the land, to take a good look at the people: were they warlike or friendly? And at the cities: were they strongly fortified? And the land itself: was the soil fertile? What crops could they plant there? Was there good pasturage for their flocks?

The young men left and returned several weeks later with their report.

"It's a good land," they told Moses. "There is good soil, and the fruit trees are full, and the vines are loaded with grapes. There is good pasturage for the flocks. You might say it's a land flowing with milk and honey. We could live there comfortably."

Moses looked carefully at the young scouts. There was something more, something that they were not telling him. He questioned them some more.

"The people are fierce," they finally told him. "Giants. Powerful warriors. And their cities are so well fortified, we'll never be able to overcome them."

Ten of the twelve scouts said that. But two of the young men felt differently. Their names were Joshua and Caleb, and they were filled with optimism and enthusiasm.

"We can do it," said Joshua, "because God is with

"THE PEOPLE ARE FIERCE."

us." Caleb agreed. They wanted to go immediately to conquer the new land that God had promised to them.

When word got around about the scouts' report, the people were afraid to go into the new land. They wanted to stay right there, in Kadesh-Barnea, and not take any chances if they had to fight the fierce giants in the Promised Land.

Moses was disappointed. He was eager to go. He himself agreed with Joshua and Caleb, the two young men who believed that with God's help they could do it. And so Moses again talked with Yahweh, seeking His guidance.

Finally, the Voice told him that the people just weren't ready. For one thing, there weren't as many young fighting men as there had been before the battle against the Amalekites. They needed more time in the desert, adjusting to their new laws, learning to live as the people of God. This generation was too pessimistic, too complaining, not deeply committed to the God who led them. Until they were ready, they should stay right where they were.

And so Moses told them of Yahweh's decision. They would stay. They would stay until a new generation of people arose who would be better prepared to go into their new land.

MOSES WAS DISAPPOINTED.

HE COULDN'T SEE IT.

16

Moses gasped for breath, his lungs wheezing with bubbling groans as he inhaled. The last mile had been torture, almost too much for a man his age.

He staggered the few remaining steps out on the top of the mountain known as Mount Nebo and looked down. From here he should be able to see the Promised Land.

But he couldn't see it. His vision was clouded over. All he saw was a misty blur, dim and hazy. He brushed the sweat from his eyes.

His knees trembling with weakness, he slid to the ground with his back against a rock. The climb had taken him almost a month. Mount Nebo was no steeper than the mountain of Sinai, which he used to climb in half a day. But that was more than forty years ago.

It had taken him thirty days to climb this small mountain. Again he gazed into the blur before him. If only he could see! This was the day the new leader Joshua planned to lead Israel across the Jordan River into the Promised Land. Moses had pushed his tired body up to the top of Mount Nebo so he could watch. Was his long, hard climb for nothing?

He squinted, concentrating all his powers on his vision. Suddenly, there it was: a brief focus on the scene before him. Gray-blue hills, fading into the distance. A snowcapped peak to the north. The Jordan River, flowing snakelike through the valley directly below him. He even saw Jericho, the first walled city Joshua would have to deal with.

And. . .yes, there they were. The vast multitude of people, slowly moving across the river. They mourned Moses' death, for when he had bid them good-bye at the foot of Mount Nebo, they had known they would not see him again. Now, though, the thirty-day period of mourning for Moses was over; Israel was on the march again.

His eyes ached from the squint, and he shut them briefly. When he opened them, the view was gone. Well, he had seen what he came to see: the Promised Land, and his people going in to conquer it.

The Promised Land truly flowed with milk and honey. He recalled the time the scouts had brought back their report of how good the land was. Over the years the beauty of the land had been talked about, with Joshua

**THERE THEY WERE,
THE VAST MULTITUDE OF PEOPLE.**

and others praising its richness, and now the people were eager to go there.

Israel had found it hard to accept Moses' decision not to go in with them. He had told them that God had forbidden him to go. That seemed to satisfy them. They would never understand that it wasn't his Promised Land. His home was back there in the desert, on the mountain the Sand Crossers called Horeb and the Egyptians, Sinai.

He shook his head sadly. He had never seen that mountain again. Forty years ago, when he left the mountain he called home, he had hoped to return. But he never did.

Well, this peak would have to do. Mount Nebo was nothing like Mount Sinai, but it was the only mountain available. He settled back on the rock and closed his eyes. This was now his home, his Promised Land.

The sun, now high in the sky, showered heat upon the rocky place on which he sat. It would be too hot soon, and he would have to move.

Suddenly he felt lonely. If only Zipporah were here! She had died last year, when fever swept the camp. The ache he felt at her passing had never gone away. He recalled the years he had spent with her: good years filled

HE FELT LONELY.

with memories. Now his sons, Gershom and Elieze, were priests of Israel.

He sighed, closing his eyes. The sun beat on the top of his head, giving him a headache and making him sweat more. He would have to seek a sheltered spot somewhere, at least until the evening breeze sprang up. But he was just too tired.

His body was fading; death must be near. But he didn't care. The face of death was friendly.

Would he meet Yahweh again when death came? He hoped so. He had met God face to face a few times in his life, and they were memorable experiences. Especially those times on Mount Sinai. If only he could go back to that mountain now. . .but he couldn't.

No. Yahweh didn't live on Mount Sinai. Those unforgettable meetings with God were high points of his life, but Yahweh had come to him on other occasions. He recalled the times he had stood before Pharaoh Ramses and felt God's power. Then there were those times in the wilderness when he had fought against the Amalekites. . . . In fact, everything he had done—every moment of every day—God had been with him. Just because he wasn't aware of the Presence at the time didn't mean . . .

He jerked himself awake. When had he gone to

HIS BODY WAS FADING.

sleep? Something had awakened him, something strange. He peered around. It was night; the day had slipped away on quiet feet. He stood up, stepping out into the cool breeze that swept across the mountain.

What had awakened him? There was no noise; he couldn't even hear the breeze. Perhaps that was what had aroused him: the silence. It was profound, majestic. . . like. . .like the silence on Mount Sinai!

Could it be? Was the Presence in this place?

Above him the stars winked at him with friendly eyes. He breathed deeply; his lungs were clear. In fact, his whole body had a youthful, vigorous feeling that he only vaguely remembered from earlier years.

He looked around. In the pale moonlight, the rocks and sandy soil seemed to glow. Beyond Mount Nebo was a deeper darkness, cool and comforting. The air was cool and clean, slightly scented by some distant fragrant blossoms.

The quiet moment continued. He could feel the silence. It seemed to enter his mind, going deeply inside him. A feeling of well-being came over him. It was familiar, and it set his blood racing and his mind tingling.

"Yahweh!" he murmured into the scented air.

He was home. Not the mountain of Sinai, nor the

WAS THE PRESENCE IN THIS PLACE!

barren desert, nor the palace in Egypt where he had spent his childhood. What he sought was here. The Presence. He had found his Promised Land.

The breeze continued to blow, silently, fragrantly, over the still form of the man on the darkened peak, rippling the white hair and beard. The eyes were closed, the wrinkles on the brown skin smoothed out, the lips composed in a quiet smile.

The stars began to fade and light crept across the peak of Mount Nebo. Soon rays from the newborn sun lightened the dusky morning, reaching down into the valley with the snakelike river. No sound intruded on the man's final resting place.

Then from a distance came the faint echo of a trumpet blaring bravely against the walls of a fortified city. Israel, too, had arrived in the Promised Land.

AUTHOR'S NOTES for Young Readers:

1. When the Suez Canal was built in 1869, it changed the geography of Egypt and Sinai. Gone were all the lakes mentioned in the Bible: the Bitter Lakes, the Reed Sea, the Lake of the Crocodiles, and other places. That's why you can't find them on a map now.

2. Most modern translators agree that the miracle of parting the waters, so the Israelites could escape from the Egyptians, probably happened at the Reed Sea, not the Red Sea. There is only one letter difference in both English and Hebrew, and the Reed Sea would probably make more sense geographically.

3. The name of God given to Moses at the burning bush is fascinating: YAHWEH. In Hebrew, it means "I AM." It can also mean "I will always be," and "I always was." In most versions of the Bible, it is translated "The Lord." Some versions say, "Jehovah." The ancient Hebrew manuscripts have just four Hebrew letters, which in English are JHVH. The English letter H is the Hebrew *alef,* but there is really no letter like it in English. It is pronounced as though you

are clearing your throat. Try saying it like this: "YECK-WECK." This is the Old Testament name for God. If you want to know the New Testament name for God, look up Philippians 2:9-11.